TEN
IRON
PRINCIPLES

TEN
IRON
PRINCIPLES

Persevering through Difficult Situations

K.A. WYPYCH

AMBASSADOR INTERNATIONAL
GREENVILLE, SOUTH CAROLINA & BELFAST, NORTHERN IRELAND
www.ambassador-international.com

Ten Iron Principles
Persevering through Difficult Situations

ISBN: 978-1-62020-870-0
eISBN: 978-1-62020-896-0

Cover Design and Interior Layout by Hannah Nichols

AMBASSADOR INTERNATIONAL
Emerald House
411 University Ridge, Suite B14
Greenville, SC 29601, USA
www.ambassador-international.com

AMBASSADOR BOOKS
The Mount
2 Woodstock Link
Belfast, BT6 8DD, Northern Ireland, UK
www.ambassadormedia.co.uk

The colophon is a trademark of Ambassador, a Christian publishing company.

Dedicated to my parents
For a lifetime of SAG

and

To Coach Grosser

CONTENTS

INTRODUCTION

ON THE ROAD TODAY FOR my ride, with sweat rolling down my face and a damp shirt clinging to my back, words flood my mind like a waterfall, pushing out all other ideas. As the empty road looms ahead of me, God pours inspiration into my soul. I plow through the miles with leg muscles swimming in lactic acid and my low back pulling taut like a drum. The words sort themselves into thoughts as the sun rises and then begins to set. I arrive home and click my GPS watch. My hamstrings and quadriceps stretch reluctantly as I cool down in my living room. Sticky with sweat, I jump in the shower. The warm water soothes the soreness away, and with wet hair, I plop on the couch with my laptop asking the heavens above, "Does God love triathlons?"

What does God have to do with triathlons, you ask? God unraveled this question for me, and the answer is, well, everything. God is about triathlons in the same way God is about every great moment in our lives, every great struggle. Unsure? Keep reading.

When I began this book, I toiled day after day with workouts from my Ironman training program crammed in before and after work. For those who may not be well versed in the art of racing, let's start with the basics. A triathlon is a competition composed of three sports. Typically, they consist of swimming, biking, and running performed in that order. An Ironman is the "big kahuna" of triathlons composed of a 2.4-mile swim, 112-mile bike, and 26.2-mile run. Some people in Hawaii hatched the idea in the 1970s, and the contest morphed into something resembling a cult.

Once while standing in the hot dog line at a minor league baseball game, I spied an Ironman tattoo on one of the guys in line. In three seconds, we became buddies; the camaraderie with Ironman is so steep. The Ironman cult. Believe it; it's real.

As I'm sure you can imagine, training for such an event takes an enormous amount of time. Enormous. Ginormous even. My life while training revolved around waking up at 4:30 a.m. for the morning workout, working 8:00 a.m. to 5:00 p.m. every day, and ended with my evening workout. My long bike rides comprised my weekends along with a few hours of sitting comatose on the couch. It was less of a life and more of a regimen. I remember changing in the bathroom of a Shell gas station once between a bike workout and a friend's wedding shower. I declined invitations to fellowship in order to be in bed by 8:30 or 9:00 p.m., and coworkers donated all of their extra food to me. I managed work, friends, God, profuse exercise, and the business end of life, such as paying bills, and I suffered multiple fits of crying face down on the carpet from the stress.

While pounding the pavement or slicing through the cool pool water with no one around except God, He inspired me to tell my story. He rewrote my life, and now I long to share His story with others. As I exercised in solitude (no friend could commit to such long miles), God's truth fluttered through my brain in bits and pieces. Over time and mile after mile, I assembled these bits into a coherent essay of sorts as I told and retold the story to myself.

Honestly, biking and running take up only twenty-five percent of my mental capacity, and I had nothing else to do. I pedaled through rural North Carolina for sixty to one hundred miles by myself week after week. While my racing fan club included a few more people, the training fan club consisted of me, my bike, and God. Writing in my head provided welcome entertainment.

I jump up and down when I think about this book being read! First, God is the awesome Giver of blessings, and I want to glorify Him and shout about His unconditional affection for all people. No relationship is able to surpass my relationship with God. I also desire to motivate people. Humanity contains more potential than we can imagine! I hope my journey inspires people who will then venture full speed after dreams and God's calling on their lives.

Second, the road to success can be longer than ninety-five miles in 106-degree heat, and I offer my encouragement and support in the form of this narrative. The Lord knows I wouldn't have survived without being buoyed by my allies. I did compete in a triathlon, but more importantly, I crossed the finish line of a struggle. I triumphed over my trial and conquered fear through my powerful God. I want everyone to move forward toward a goal with God as their cheerleader.

Third, I owe my family and friends a trillion-dollar debt for all of their love and support, which I never deserved. Stress, perseverance, and endurance encourage long-term growth but can elicit crying, screaming, and tantrums. Like oil or wine, I needed refinement.

Fourth, I long for roads free from drivers who seem delighted to run me over. Exercise fanatics pay taxes, too, and we need the world's compassion! The next time readers drive past a runner, I hope they say a prayer for the athlete's safety and success while training. Or, even better, I pray patience spreads and people grow to stifle annoyance when they see a cyclist on the road. Or best yet, I implore drivers to give bikers a little extra room and avoid the dangerous "squeeze by." The car "squeeze by" routine, where vehicles give riders only few inches as they pass, exists. I've wobbled from automobile gusts and had side mirrors only inches from my body whiz past me at sixty miles an hour.

Everyone around us holds onto hopes, dreams, and goals. Remember that. People in our paths are not merely detours in our day. We need to stop and actually look at people. I struggled on that bike, on those long rides. I left my heart out on those roads. I am optimistic that at the end of this, my readers will bond with me and wave at every cyclist they see, just in case it's me. I hope my readership smiles when they see God work in my life, in their own lives, and in the lives of those around them.

When the essay or story first formed in my quieted brain as my body pumped muscles from flexion to extension, I had no plans to write it down, to rein in my thoughts with structured grammar. Then a guy in my small group at church asked me to speak about perseverance and my Ironman training experience. I'm not perfect, and as I alluded to earlier, I didn't endure this whole training thing very well. The stress was a catalyst for some of the more unpolished parts of my personality, and I acted like a toddler at times. I'm a sinner trying to be obedient. I did write it on paper, and I did share.

Now, I recount the journey which completely changed my life. This is the story of how I came to love God, and how He completely transformed me. My greatest dream in all of this is that if you don't know Jesus, you will meet Him here.

The story ends exactly as it begins:

My name is Kelly, and I'm an Ironman.

PART ONE

THE BEGINNING

CHAPTER 1
PRECURSOR

AS SOMEONE WHO LOVES ORGANIZATION and structure, I will start at the beginning. I was born in Michigan, lived in a small town, and had a nice family. I'm the middle child with an older sister and a younger brother. I suffer from middle child syndrome, blaming my siblings for all of our squabbles as any middle child ought to do. Among my earliest memories, my family called me stubborn. Not sweet, not nice, not lovely, not beautiful. Stubborn. I believe they nearly hit the bull's-eye but instead landed just outside the mark. I view myself as perseverant, tenacious, and relentless rather than stubborn.

My brother and sister liked the same toys and played similar games, which cemented the two to one dynamic. So really, I had no other choice. I grew into a little fighter. I learned very early on how to battle for what I wanted even against the odds. Granted, we fought over who played with the Legos, but still. At least this is the way I remember it, although my brother and sister might say otherwise.

Nothing takes one back to childhood behaviors like time spent with a little brother. His wife thanks me when I visit them because he stops picking on her. He needles me repeatedly to this day, pushing my buttons until I want to scream. It's funny how portions of our family relationships stay rooted in the past, and we react in predictable patterns simply because that's the way we've always done it. But I digress.

Admittedly, my characteristic of "being stubborn" has not always served me well. I have a tough time putting down a terrible book or turning off a bad movie. With enough time and effort, most things can be finished. However, this perspective is not without cost. My stubbornness is rooted in pride; I don't enjoy how quitting reflects on me. I have made bad decisions as an adult simply because I refused to quit. I also have judged others based on their lack of perseverance and generated self-righteous tendencies as a result.

An Ironman triathlon is a feat of athleticism, which is why it's so shocking that I'm involved in this story. I remember my first bike. I gravitated to the light blue color and the comfort of the white banana seat. But, I loved the rainbow decal on the down tube, and I had to have it. Who chooses a bike because of the sticker? (My dad once bought a car because of the radio, so the apple doesn't fall far from the tree).

All the neighborhood kids learned to ride before I did. I felt nervous I wouldn't be able to master the "balance" thing, and I didn't want to have everyone see me fall on the ground. I practiced on our family "training bike," an old red bike with a very hard seat. I recall the first feeling of success as I pedaled (after tottering for a few seconds) away from my dad with the wind blowing my hair.

Unfortunately, my untold athletic prowess ends here. As a youth, I competed in recreational softball, and my dad coached the team. I frequently played catcher because no one else wanted the position. Rather than listen to the other kids and their parents complain, my dad stuck me behind the plate. After nearly every pitch, I conversed with the umpire as I rose from my squatting position to retrieve the ball I had just missed. Sometimes the umpire would grab a loose ball to save me the trip. My belief is they secretly rooted for me to improve; everyone loves an underdog. However, I stayed in the bottom third of competitors for all of high school.

Though I'm stubborn and have little athletic ability, teachers always lauded me for being a smart kid. I earned a "C" in handwriting in first grade, much to my dismay. My parents were very disappointed, and I didn't like how the "C" looked alongside the other "A's" and "B's" on my report card. I worked harder after that, bending my head right down to the paper to ensure my cursive letters were within the lines.

I became a straight "A" student and excelled at my schoolwork. I like succeeding, what can I say? I never got another "C."

In school I processed the information faster than the other kids and moved through the questions and assignments before anyone around me. Often, I clarified the statements made by the teacher, turning to the students sitting near me to articulate the concepts in different words so they would understand. My success in the classroom fueled my "performance driven" mentality.

In high school I played volleyball for two years and was mediocre at best. One day the coach met me in the hallway and walked me to class with his arm resting lightly on my shoulders. He explained in a quiet voice that volleyball may not be my thing. My sister had been a solid volleyball player, but, again, I wasn't much of an athlete. I accepted this rejection fairly well. I realized the other girls were simply better than I.

I played softball in high school as well. I loved playing second base, but another girl surpassed me in skill, so I played back-up for second base or in left field. In fast pitch softball, not a lot of balls end up in left field. One time we practiced indoors in the gymnasium, and I missed a ground ball. Coach Venia yelled at me, "You've got a 3.9 grade point average and you can't even field a d— ball." Afterwards, the coaches always called me three-nine as a nickname. It hurt some, but I felt shielded by my academic successes.

I had amazing times and great opportunities in my youth. I try to accurately confront the brutal facts of my everyday life, sometimes successfully and sometimes not. The brutal facts of my mostly pleasant and greatly nurturing childhood remained unchanged. I was a good kid. I was a smart kid. I had a good life. My siblings were pains in ways all siblings are, but otherwise they were great. I was mediocre at team sports. I was tenacious even at a young age. These facts formed the foundation of my life.

CHAPTER 2

FRIDAY NIGHT LIGHTS

THE STAGE IS SET WITH some idea of how I was molded in my young life, my innate level of athletic skill, and the intensity of my tenacity. Now, it gets a little more interesting. I was well-known or maybe infamous in my high school, but not from what you'd think looking in from the cheap seats. I was second in my class, voted most likely to succeed, and class brain. I lived as a super nerd, which probably caused me to blend in more than stand out. However, I became the talk of the town when, during my sophomore year in high school, I became the first girl in my high school to play on the boys' football team.

My hometown, Marysville, MI, was a football town at the time. There were 160-plus in my graduating class and something like sixty to eighty guys on the varsity football squad. On Friday nights, students watched football and went to the dance afterwards. The town had a population of 12,000, and there wasn't much else to do. Football was what happened on Friday night. Once when I was in middle school, the football team won the state title, and there was a street sign on the outskirts of town which read, "Last one out of Marysville, turn out the lights." A girl on the football team broached borderline sacrilegious.

It all started at the Marysville/Port Huron Northern football game, the last game of the season in my freshman year. I sat with my sister, Wendy, and her friend on a Friday night watching the game at Port Huron Stadium. I loved (and still love) watching football outdoors at night. The quarterback's performance was a disaster. I remember he dropped back in the pocket once and slipped and fell with no defenders close to him. Our offense played atrocious that year.

As I watched and cheered near the end of the game, I mentioned that football looked like a lot of fun to play. My sister's friend said she had wanted to play but never considered trying. I sat stunned. Thoughts ran through my mind about how I wanted to live my life with gumption. What was a life if filled only with fear and missed opportunities? Sure, I wasn't very good at volleyball or softball, but at least I tried. Hauntingly, pictures of an empty life flashed in my mind's eye as I perched on my bleacher no longer seeing what was on the field in front of me. Then a bit of dread began to set in as a question started filling my brain and pressing up against my skull on all sides. *What kind of effort would it take?*

With a sense of adventure welling up in my gut, I remember declaring to Wendy and her friend how I should go out for the football team, so I could learn to play. My sister said a girl couldn't play on the boys' football team. *Well, that's not right*, I thought, *could they stop me?* The gears in my head turned like mad. I pondered whether they could legally keep me from playing, but somehow, I doubted it. Wouldn't that be discrimination?

The possible discrimination against women angle got my blood boiling and bolstered my courage. *I should be able to try this. I can try this. I should try this. I will never know unless I do.* If my quest became derailed due to school policy, then so be it. But the dream wasn't going to die with me. That was for other people.

Many people in Marysville speculated about why I went out for the football team. Some people reasoned I wanted to prove that girls are as capable as boys. Some decided I rebelled against the system. My dad even told me in later years he felt it was to compete with my sister's volleyball skills and success, so I could bathe in the spotlight for a change. Deep down in my unconscious, some truth may exist in all of those motives. In my heart though, none of those arguments resonated.

Honestly, there was little to no feminist motivation driving my two-year stint on the junior varsity high school football team. I was the smartest girl in my class; I knew I could compete with boys. I studied science, and men's bodies are built differently than women. They have more muscular strength. I wasn't trying to undo God's handiwork. At my core resided the two reasons I tried out for the football team: I thought it would be fun to play, and I wasn't going to let fear dictate my life. I didn't want to be limited by the minds and fears of others or of myself.

On the flip side, I won't lie; the fact that many people conveyed I couldn't play football did, at times, fuel the fire already burning. An inner voice occasionally shouted, *who do you think you are telling me what I can or cannot do?* But overall, I wanted to be anonymous and play football. It was never about what other people thought. If this had been the case, I wouldn't have played at all! The brutal facts of self-assessment here are that I was never very good at football nor did I ever believe I would be. I didn't play for glory. I didn't play because I was an exceptional athlete. I didn't play to prove a point. I played because I thought it would be a fun, worthwhile experience. I wanted to be out on the grass under the stadium lights, and I wasn't going to let my fears or others' doubts stop me.

CHAPTER 3

FLAGSTONES

I BEGAN TO INQUIRE AS to which gate keepers I needed to speak with regarding this new football frontier. Everyone eyeballed me like I was crazy, which increased my self-doubt. My fears encompassing the task at hand frequently produced pounding heart palpitations and episodes of uncontrolled sweating. I had meetings with the principal and a couple of lower echelon coaches. Before every meeting, my pulse would be thrashing in my ears and I would feel blood rushing into my face like Class IV rapids. Eventually, I was advised I needed to meet with the Head Varsity Football Coach, Walt Braun.

Now this was serious business. People did not trifle with Coach Braun. Unless one grows up in an area that values old-school high school football, they may not comprehend the quality of man Coach Braun represented. He was legendary in the history of Marysville High School football. He personified Marysville High School football. He was tough as nails, a man to fear, a man to respect. He wore polyester shorts and the tube socks pulled up to his knees, but no one would even conceive of teasing him. He had a whistle, and he knew how to use it. He had a mouth like a sailor; he would cuss players out if they weren't playing hard enough. I'm sure he made at least a few of the boys cry.

In later years he suffered a stroke which made him a bit less scary because he walked with a cane and lost quite a bit of weight, but he still was a tough, hard-hitting man. The school district ultimately fired him after he hit some kid with his cane for messing up a play. Regardless, he is an unparalleled legend in my eyes and in the eyes of many in Marysville.

I met with Coach Braun in his office to discuss the steps I needed to take to try out for the football team. I could barely hear my own voice as my heartbeat filled the room. I tried not to shake and sweat poured down my back and underarms. He terrified me. After I announced my intent to play football, he laughed at me though not directly outright (but close). He explained to me with a smirk on his face how I would need to attend the football team meeting in the spring and I would have to participate in the Dirty Dozen. At least he didn't say, "No."

The Dirty Dozen consisted of a three-week conditioning camp at the end of August before official football practices began. There was an hour-long session in the mornings and a session in the evenings, Monday through Thursday. Athletes needed to attend any twelve sessions in order to earn a T-shirt which said, "I Survived the Dirty Dozen." The training periods were known for being incredibly grueling experiences. Coach Braun informed me if I successfully completed the Dirty dozen, then we could talk about my football aspirations. I simply said, "Okay," and high-tailed it out of there.

Within days, I felt brave, knowing that the next challenge was months away. Time shields us from fear. I shared my intent to play football matter-of-factly with my friends in class and outside of school, and most of them were supportive to my face.

But time dwindled, and, eventually I made my appearance at the junior varsity football team meeting in the spring. None of the guys would sit next to me on the wooden bleachers in the gymnasium. I was mortified, but I couldn't blame them. I forced myself not to look at the others but to look straight ahead and keep breathing. Lance, who was a student in some honors classes with me, had pity on my ostracization and sat near me. He spoke kindly; he was a nice guy and sensed my pain. Other football players stared and snickered; I tried not to notice.

People know when they're weird; they feel it. I felt it. Actually, I don't think certain people are weird and others are normal. We're all weird in our own little secret, peculiar ways. The difference is some of us aren't afraid of it. So, I sat there, embracing my weirdness, yet trying to blend in with the wood of the bleacher seats. I couldn't become upset. I counseled myself through it, *just look down, look like you don't care, and keep breathing. Fake it until you make it.*

The meeting commenced, thankfully, and everyone focused on the coach. Coach Grosser was the principal of the school, and I had already spoken with him briefly. He was intimidating but he was much more approachable than Coach Braun. He was a tough, big man, but he had a kind heart and it showed. He played offensive line in college (if it was defensive line, he's going to kill me!). For readers unfamiliar with football, the offensive and defensive lines are separate units composed of the big guys who line up on opposite sides of the line, crashing head-on into one another after the ball is hiked.

He stood in front of the bleachers discussing the composition of a successful football team, and he questioned the attendees regarding goals we had established for ourselves as football players. We wrote these goals down and submitted them. I'm not exactly certain what I wrote, but it was probably something along the lines of, "make it through the season."

Coach Grosser knew I would be in attendance. During the meeting, he commented on how we had to be willing to put everything on the line and used me as a quick example. I'm sure it would have been difficult to completely avoid the topic of my presence. I stuck out as the only girl.

Thankfully, I wasn't the only person out of place. There was a guy, Ryan, from a nearby town who was at the meeting, too. His family re-located, he would be playing football at Marysville. He stood up boldly in his reddish-purple colored long-sleeved T-shirt (I have this uncanny ability to remember what people wear) and introduced himself. This caused more of a stir than my presence as he hailed from a competing team. He was the enemy. Ryan sat in the front row and spoke in a loud voice while I tried my hardest to slink into the background and said nothing. He wasn't tall, but I'll be darned if he wasn't one of the fastest, scrappiest halfbacks around. Incidentally, when Ryan submitted his goal for the year, it said, "State Champs '92."

After the meeting ended, I breathed a deep sigh of relief. I have no hesitation standing up for what I want or against things I know are wrong, but it's not a good feeling to be an outcast, to be shunned by all in the room. It's an awful feeling. But, I did what I needed to do. Doing the right thing, in life or for myself, is a choice. I shrink from cheating myself, cheating others, or letting someone without a voice be cheated. So, I gather my courage and do what needs to be done. That's why I went to the meeting. I wanted to play football, and this meeting was a step along my road. But I'd be lying if I said it wasn't nice to head back to my regular life and blend into the student body milling in the hallway.

As I continued to apprise people of my football desires and goals, they either weren't surprised or didn't take me seriously. I couldn't be concerned with the reactions of others. I lifted weights and ran at the track during the spring and summer. I didn't know much (or anything) about weights, but I tried. My days of regimented preparation developed as an adult through years of disciplined pursuits.

The Dirty Dozen commenced in August. I had nausea at the very thought of it. Truth be told, I experienced a great deal of nausea over the next several years. I never vomited; it was more like feeling perpetually queasy. I had to drum up courage every day during football season. It never felt easy or comfortable. It did get better and more familiar, but the game challenged me physically and internally.

Dirty Dozen workouts started with a distance run of 800 meters followed by ten to fifteen stadium step repetitions and then wind sprints. The first 800 was a killer. I wasn't a distance runner at this point and everyone ran so fast. Some seemed like they sprinted the whole way! Guys tried to best other guys, and everyone tried to keep up with the Joneses. As the first part of the workout, everyone charged out of the gates on fresh legs.

Next came the stadium steps, which were my favorite, going up one side of the bleachers, over, down, over, up, over, down, run around and repeat. They weren't easy. We worked our way from ten to twelve to fifteen reps, increasing the increments during each of the three weeks. I liked the repetition of this drill. Systematically executing a repetitive motion while slowly dismantling the goal at hand satisfies something in me. Piece by piece, bleacher by bleacher, step by step. I was too out of shape then to appreciate the steady running portion of each session.

I swear during every workout, someone would puke. The boys couldn't pace themselves, never wanting to be beat. I had it easier since no one expected me to succeed, and my bar was set pretty low. We ran on the former, legendary Viking Stadium bleachers. Everyone struggled with fatigued muscles as sweat dripped off their legs with every footfall.

The sprints were my least favorite because I'm slow. If someone hadn't puked during the stadium steps, then they did during the sprints. Coach Braun ran us to death. I relished the shuffles and grapevines as they allowed me to catch my breath somewhat. Coaches timed us in the 40-yard dash on several occasions, and my time was 6.3 seconds. All of you footballers out there know how slow this is. No Usain Bolt here.

The Thursday workout was different from Monday through Wednesday and consisted of something called Commando-ball. All the guys loved this workout, but I hated it. It was a bunch of guys running around playing a cross between dodgeball and rugby. Basically, the contest was too much testosterone and not enough rules. There wasn't a role or position for me to play, so I hung out by the goal and played cherry picker or defense. I tolerated it. I did what was needed to finish and get my shirt.

Three weeks of steps and sprints and commando-ball and steps and sprints and commando-ball and steps and sprints and commando-ball. And you betcha, I got my shirt. Coach Braun was surprised I survived. I can't blame him; I was 5′5″ and weighed 127 pound. I was the smallest, weakest, and one of the slowest people on the field. But not everyone made it to twelve sessions. Not everyone completed the Dirty Dozen. I did. Score one point for the small, slow, weird chick. Holla!

What I didn't know during this time was my parents had multiple meetings with school officials, including the coaches, principal, and the superintendent. Completing the Dirty Dozen was a sign this was going to be bigger than they thought. Everyone had hoped I would just go away. After I succeeded at the two hurdles set before me by Coach Braun, I wondered if the school board/administrators relied on my parents to prohibit me from playing.

I had two things going for me on this front. First, I was a stubborn fifteen-year-old high school girl. I'm sure my parents knew how histrionically relentless I would be if they crushed my dream. My mom and dad would never have heard the end of my devastation as I sulked and moaned incessantly while traipsing around the house. Oh, how I could (and can) sulk! I'm sure they dreaded the possibility.

That's not the primary reason, though, as I've sulked about many other things and have not gotten my way. The main reason they didn't stop me was because they wanted to give me the freedom to become my own person. They wanted me to be *me*. My parents desired that I grow into the person God shaped me to be.

My mom said they didn't want me to look back at never getting the chance to play football with regret due to a choice they made. If I didn't make it on my own, they would have handed me Kleenexes (they have always been there to hand me tissues). I had their support if I failed, but they didn't want to be the cause of my failure. Throughout my life, in many more situations than can be recounted, my parents have let me be me. They don't always agree with my decisions or understand my choices, but they've never tried to hold me back from being who I felt led to be. They've loved me regardless of what I've been doing, which is why this book is dedicated to them. I don't know if I've ever loved anyone or anything as unconditionally as my parents love me.

In the end the school decided it had no legal leg to stand on if I decided to sue them, so they let me play. Nearly everyone involved was a bit dismayed at this decision, even a part of me. Like I said, courage is not the absence of fear but the unwillingness to let it derail you. If they had told me no, I could have walked away with my head held high. But that didn't happen, so I tried out for the football team. As the start of football season approached, terror ensued as my palms sweated consistently and the heart palpitations occurred on a regular basis. Before, it had just been the precursor stuff. Sure, the previous hurdles were scary, but this was it. Holy cow. What on earth was I thinking?

CHAPTER 4
PRACTICE

THE SEASON BEGAN WITH AN equipment day where the staff fit players with pads, helmet, etc. and assigned lockers. I noticed every noise and the hairs on my neck stood on end as my sense of awareness seemed heightened. In my gut, I felt suspense akin to watching a horror movie. The coaches provided me with equipment like the other guys. They gave me shoulder pads which came down over my chest for "protection" of my breasts (though no one would say it directly). Getting fitted for a helmet was difficult as, apparently, I have a small head. I ended up receiving an old helmet with the Viking wings (really horns but we called them wings) on the side. My jersey number was 27. Most receivers wore higher numbers, but this was one of the numbers that wasn't taken in my size. Most receivers aren't 127 pounds, I guess.

Coach Grosser set me up in the girls' locker room with a locker nearest a bolted side door to the boys' locker room no one used. This way coach could slide the practice schedule under the door for me each day. He posted the itinerary in the boys' locker room, but I couldn't go in there. He looked into my locker once where everything was neatly hung and washed weekly. He said it was the cleanest and tidiest football locker he had ever seen.

I had trouble with the playbook. It didn't make sense to me right away. I tried to study the plays and memorize them before coach explained the "system" to me. They didn't have to describe it to the guys as they had been playing under the system for years. I couldn't believe I struggled with the intellectual part of football. I mean, I excelled at learning! It was the actual football playing I was supposed to grapple with!

Coach decided to position me at split end as a wide receiver because he thought I knew something about split ends as a girl (can you believe it?). Who ever heard of a 5'5" wide receiver? Once I understood the system, it was simple. Each back/receiver had a number as did each space between the linemen and each pass route. In the system I was the "2" receiver. The quick pass route was a "7." So, a "27" was the split end going for a quick pass. A "42" was the half back, who was number "4," running up the middle through the "2" hole, which is a specific gap between two linemen. There were other descriptors like Tripp's, when the receivers doubled up on one side. Other code words indicated we would line up in reverse on the line and each play was given on a specific count. Overall, the plays were self-explanatory. Before I grasped it, Coach Grosser told me, "You'll get this. If all the boys can learn it, you surely can."

Everyone had their place in the huddle; it wasn't willy-nilly. I stood in the same place in the huddle each time. The QB would get the play from coach and then tell the huddle, "44 on two, 44 on two, break" and we would all slap our thigh pads and head to the line. Because of these types of coding systems, a quarterback can call an audible and change the play at the line. (I hope the light goes on for at least one person here).

The football team had strict rules. Hair could not stick down below the bottom of the helmet. No one had to ask me to cut my hair. I didn't want to cause any additional issues above and beyond my presence on the team. I was also sure they would kick me off the team if given the chance. I had my hair cut into a bob which fit under my helmet. I was shy about telling the stylist at the *Hair Stop* that I was on the football team, but I needed to ensure she cut it short enough. I also knew I could no longer paint my nails. What kind of wide receiver has pink fingernails? But I did start painting my toenails. I painted them bright red to remind me of my femininity. Though I played on a guys' team, I was still a girl, and it was good and okay to be a girl, even if only in some secret way.

For the first several days, we showed up in football cleats (which I still have in my "memoir box") and helmets without pads. We ran non-contact drills and plays to get loose and warmed up. Eventually, the day came when we had to suit up and actually hit one another. In Marysville the first day of hitting practice is called "Christmas."

I'm not sure if other high school football teams have "Christmas." I'm not sure where the name came from but that's what the first day of hitting practice is called. Some of the big football fans in the town would come, stand on the sidelines, and watch the varsity team on Christmas. The players strung Christmas trees from the goal posts and piled them around the field. It was a ritual. Guys who were good, strong athletes and who had held back their aggression for a whole year were now prepared to release it (Incredible Hulk style) on the opposing player.

I just wanted to get it over with. I wanted my first big hit, so I could check that box. Talk about fear. I had no idea about what it would be like to be the smallest person on the field and have everyone waiting to wax me for invading their territory.

So "Christmas" came, and I suited up. We ran passing drills, and I went for the ball and got tackled. The grass rose up very quickly to meet me as a defender (Billy) pulled me to the ground. And you know what? It didn't hurt. I wore so much padding, the tackle mildly jarred me if that.

Although the guys probably did want to flatten me, I also think they were afraid of hitting me too hard. It was difficult for them. Some teammates had been taught to respect women (not all of them for sure), and they didn't know how to handle it. I don't blame them and appreciate all they went through for me.

Don't get me wrong, getting tackled can hurt sometimes. Once I caught a pass and a defensive back tackled me immediately. I landed on my stomach with the ball crushing into my gut underneath me. Man, falling on the ball hurts and makes it really hard to breathe. I also ached when my head hit the ground before my body, which is known in football circles as "getting your bell rung." On those occasions, I walked dazed back to the huddle. Those types of hits do happen, but they are the exception, not the norm. Most of the hits are tolerable and just part of the game. For full disclosure, I was a sophomore on the junior varsity team. It may be different in varsity and college.

The first test of the season was the "Blue and White Scrimmage." The teams (varsity, junior varsity, and freshman) divided into two strings of offensive and defensive platoons, which played against one another. It wasn't a game, really, but the scrimmage was the first football event. The entrance fee was one bar of soap. I guess the boys used the soap.

Prior to the start of the game, we took team and individual pictures. My cheerleader friends came up and had their picture taken with me. For our individual pictures, each of us would put one knee on the ground next to a helmet. We used my helmet as it had the Viking horns already painted on the sides. Everyone else would get Viking horn stickers placed on their helmets after the scrimmage. The scrimmage was an initiation.

It felt like an out of body experience to be standing in a football uniform among the guys. I wasn't very comfortable. In practice, at least, I was just a member of the team, which was still atypical. But there, in public, with my helmet off, I was on display for all to see. This was my battle, my goal, my dream, and I didn't need an audience. Everyone seemed to stare at me. For future games, I always left my helmet on if it was at all possible. I preferred to stay hidden.

My memory of the actual scrimmage is limited. I'm a girl so I'm missing the "play by play memory gene" that so many men (at least my brother) seem to have. When talking about college or professional football, my brother will always say, "Don't you remember that play by *no longer remember his name* in that game against *no real recollection*?"

"No, I don't remember."

"How can you not remember that?," he queries completely dismayed. Then it's my turn to be perturbed. My brother and I have repeated this same conversation a half-dozen times, and yet he can't seem to remember I won't recall one obscure play years ago by a player whose name I no longer know!

So, for those male athletic junkies who hoped for detailed play by play accounts of my football efforts, I'm so sorry to disappoint. I remember how I felt during my experience; after all, I am a girl. I played a small amount that day and afterwards felt solid with the scrimmage under my belt. It was hot in August in full pads. I was still a fish out of water, unsure of what the season would bring.

CHAPTER 5

THE SEASONS

THROUGHOUT MY TWO SEASONS, I played in about half of the games. We had to be significantly winning or losing for me to enter a game, and I usually went in during the fourth or sometimes the third quarter. I didn't care. I wasn't very good, and I didn't expect the team to sacrifice winning for me. Not everything is about being good. Sometimes it's just about being.

Playing football may sound like more of an ordeal than a rewarding experience, but it wasn't. I had oodles of fun and fulfillment even though internal and external drama encircled me like a tornado. I had the best time. I love football and all of the little details, like the smell of the grass at night (I swear it smells different at night!), the look of the stadium lights against a dark sky, the pregame ritual, and the smacking of thigh pads out of a huddle break on the field. I loved the "Viking Huddle" where all team members run and jump up over a certain player creating a standing pile of players all reaching their hands toward the center. The feeling of running out of the tunnel at the start of a game is second to none. If you've never ran out of a tunnel into the lights and onto a football field while people cheered, and the fight song blared, you missed out. I wouldn't trade it for anything. These memories are perfectly framed moments from a movie, which cause tears to well up in my eyes. Whatever else you might think about high school football, to me it's all of these things.

I loved game day. Everyone wore ties. I wore dress pants and a shirt. I may have worn a few skirts, but I tried not to draw attention to myself as a girl. After school, we dressed in our game day uniforms.

Usually, we practiced in white pants and mesh shirts. Game shirts and pants were nice, made of thick, shiny material. The Viking uniform had navy blue "home" jerseys and white "away" jerseys paired with gray pants with navy pinstripes down the sides. We wore white socks and gray helmets. Before meeting up with the boys, I would lie on a bench and listen to my Walkman in the girls' locker room. Yes, cassette tapes. I flipped the tape back and forth between two songs because of the way they fell on the tape. Every game day was the same. "You Shook Me All Night Long" by ACDC and "Unchained Melody" by the Righteous Brothers. I know, I know, the Righteous Brothers? But that's what it was. For better or for worse, I listened to these two songs repeatedly before every game. They still hold a special place in my heart.

Once in uniform, we trekked down into the basement to the cement hallways between the locker rooms and the weight room. The coaching staff turned the lights off, and we would lie on the ground and prepare. It was dark and silent. No music, no Walkmans, no talking. We quietly rallied our momentum and focused on the goal. Winning. Doing our best. Putting it all out there on the field for the team. The energy was palpable as it heightened, filling the air like static electricity as I lay there in the dark with my teammates, getting mentally ready for the challenges ahead.

I never caught a pass in a game or scored a touchdown. The quarterback usually overthrew the ball and, not many pass plays were called my way. I didn't play until the third game, which was against Richmond. I can still smell the grass. We faced the goalpost in front of the junior high around the twenty to thirty yard line. I threw a couple of blocks (or tried to), and we ended up scoring on the drive. My heart soared, and the offense cheered on the field. I made it through and into a game. Can you imagine? Red toenails and all, I was a football player. My friend, who gave me a mug with a picture of me in uniform (which I still have), was on the sidelines as a cheerleader, and her mom signaled to her that I was in the game.

Let me step up on my soapbox for a minute. Sometimes people miss out on life because they use someone else's standards as a baseline for their own goals. By every other player's standard, I was a failure. I barely played, was unexceptional when I did play, and never scored any points. I also had a limp from a pulled muscle. When I ran, a few people called me "hop along." The sum does not equal success if measured by any other player's measuring stick.

I caution you to stay in your own lane when evaluating your life and goals. Pay no attention to the cars in the lane beside yours. No one else has been in your particular circumstances with your particular resources. No one has been built quite like you with your gifts, talents, faults, and weaknesses. Be you to the best of your ability. I was never going to be a star football player, and that was never the goal. To BE a football player was the goal. And after that game, I was one.

There were several memorable moments involving various locker rooms. Understandably, there wasn't a girls' locker room under the football stadium. To the left of the tunnel was one room for the offense and to the right, one for the defense. I never thought about the meetings which must have occurred to figure out the logistics of adding a female to the mix. There must have been many.

When we ran into the tunnel at halftime, the boys would all cram into the left room, so I could use the bathroom in the other. Once everyone's "business" was taken care of, I went in with the offense, and the defense went into the room with my bathroom. The boys had to be protected from being seen by me, and I had to be protected from being seen by them. The inherent difficulty in this never crossed my mind! There had to be a game plan for our halftime! The coaches gave good pep talks, but they seemed really short. Maybe it was due to the halftime bathroom logistics. Maybe halftime seems longer when sitting in the stands.

Though I was a girl and one of his favorites, Coach still screamed at me in practice on occasion. In one instance, I ran a "2" route apparently incorrectly, and he yelled at me. "You're not even running hard, and you're not in the right location. Last year you could run it fine but now you can't. Get back out there." He shoved me to the front of the line again to run my route. I liked pass routes. I thought I was doing it right. It's funny, though I felt frustrated because I didn't know what he wanted, getting shouted at made me feel part of the team.

Down-ups were the evilest of evil. Come on, some of you must be familiar with down-ups. They don't look difficult when watching someone else do them, but they are killers. A down-up is when a player stands in a slightly crouched position hopping back and forth rapidly from one foot to the other and then drops on their chest to the ground (in full pads) and then pops back up. We used to idle back and forth, and the coaches would blow a whistle and we all dropped as a team with a collective air expelling grunt, and then popped back up only to repeat the process.

The only thing worse than down-ups was a string of down-ups done on every 5-yard line marker, called a crab-belly. I was late to practice one time with several other guys, and we were assigned a 50-yard crab-belly to make up for being tardy. It never looked tough when others executed one, but this was grueling. As we were finishing and approaching the 50-yard line, we could barely get up off the ground. And this was only a half crab-belly! My hair had shifted over my face in my helmet, so I couldn't see. My legs felt like jelly, and instead of dropping to my chest, I collapsed from exhaustion at each line. And I wasn't alone. The other guys were in the same brutal boat. Coach made his point loud and clear. I wasn't late again.

In my second year, we went to Croswell-Lexington High School or CrosLex as it was called. They didn't have a locker room, so our team congregated under their goal post in full view of the other team and the fans in the stands. I never took my helmet off. With it on, I resembled a puny player. With my helmet off, I looked like a girl. I wore a headband under my helmet to keep the hair out of my face. Taking my helmet off would make a spectacle of myself among the crowds walking by on the way to the concession stands. It was a warm evening, and my head was hot inside the helmet. A few of the other players kept their helmets on, too, though no one was instructed to do so. I like to think they did it in solidarity. I was extremely conscious of the people striding by who glanced at the team. There's no way they could have known, but I was still paranoid.

Another locker room experience happened back on my home turf in the girls' locker room. I trudged in from practice, tired and dirty, dressed in full gear. The visiting girls' basketball team always shared the locker room I was in. They were involved in their pre-game routine and attempted to get psyched up by chanting. Voices petered off as heads rotated to check out the girl football player walking in and taking off all her equipment.

One basketballer asked me, "Do you play football?"

The sarcasm in my mind dripped like sweat. "No, I always dress like this," I wanted to say. I carried a helmet and wore pads, for crying out loud. Instead, I answered, "yes."

"Is there a girls' football team?"

"No."

"You play on the guys' team?"

"Yes." Then I banged around in my locker to show we were finished. I get that it was a shocker to people and no one knew. But I was tired and hungry and didn't want to have to explain myself. It was weird being the only girl on the football field to come into the locker room and be the only football player in the women's locker room. I later wondered if the interruption affected their game.

CHAPTER 6

INNER TURBULENCE

EVERYONE REMEMBERS THINGS DIFFERENTLY. ONE of the players told his girlfriend I didn't play hard and tried to get out of drills. I don't remember it this way. I hated certain drills, like the Split T drill. In this exercise, one offensive lineman faced off against one defensive lineman and a running back or receiver tried to run past the defenseman based on the offensive block. It's football at its most primal level.

I got waxed repeatedly. I threw a couple of good blocks against boys who were afraid of hurting me, but I don't think that counts against their football skill. Maybe my friend's boyfriend was right. But I stood in line after line of drills waiting to get demolished and taking my turn. Was I excited about drills where the other guys would crush me? No. Maybe that showed. But I got tackled more than most due to lack of speed and strength, so I took my share of punishment.

Due to the difficulty for me in some of the drills, I had a very visceral response to impending football practices. During the last hour of class every day, my palms would start to get sweaty and my heart would race in anticipation and fear of the afternoon practice to come. It was hard. I was terrible at football. Though the tackles don't really hurt, nobody looks forward to getting their butt kicked. Practices for sports typically aren't much fun at baseline; I was the worst player on the team, so it was even worse.

A dichotomy existed. A season of football embodied moments I loved and moments I dreaded. I chose to pursue my desire to play. I grabbed hold of it and wouldn't let go. But I'm not invincible. I still was afraid. I felt fear, but I was determined not to be controlled by it.

45

Some people are carefree because they don't recognize the danger. I recognized the peril, but instead, I chose to focus on the end goal and the experience of playing football despite my fears. I faced my fear every day of the season. I refused to let it stop me.

As an inferior player in skill and stature, I felt guilty for letting people down. If a back was running behind my block, sometimes he was crushed. Ryan, the guy who had made his presence known at the pre-season football team meeting, yelled at me in a game once because I missed my block against a 6-plus foot defensive end and Ryan was hit hard. I tried, and I missed. No one likes to feel they let people down. I have pride! No one likes to perform poorly. But I wasn't going to let it beat me. I kept trying. As luck would have it, Ryan's scolding improved my blocking as my anger for being singled out rose to the surface.

The point is some goals in life are difficult. Most things worthwhile have a cost attached to them. Sometimes Satan tries to knock us off our paths using fear as a detour. Fulfilling dreams takes hard work, sacrifice, and humility. Often, these aspirations bring the best experiences in life. The rewards we earn. The battles we fight. The victories we win. Remember, everyone loves an underdog.

Our culture elevates immediate gratification above long-term growth and accomplishment. The big picture takes hard work, and it's called "hard work" because that's what it is. I wouldn't have my life today if I hadn't sacrificed for the bigger goals or laid myself on the line. I would have missed out on some of the most valuable experiences of my life. The challenge is to exchange what you can have today for who you can be tomorrow.

I sat out only one practice for being sick. I had a cold, felt dizzy, and had bad cramps. When I went to put my pads on, I almost fell. So, I didn't practice and felt oddly sad yet relieved. Coach had told me before the season that if I ever felt like I faced an injury, it was okay if I sat out. He said, "I will never be able to forgive myself if you can't have children one day because of something I let happen to you on the field." He advised, "You just tell me, no questions asked." But, this isn't why I skipped one practice. I sat on the sidelines because I was sick, but I experienced genuine concern for my well-being from the coaching staff.

People ask if my breasts hurt when I got tackled. The answer is no. My abdomen hurt when I landed on the ball, knocking the wind out of me. My head hurt on the rare occasion when my helmet hit the ground hard. The remaining tackles involved landing on the grass without issue. This brings me to the most important question which no one has ever asked me about football. But . . . and this is a big but (guys, feel free to skip ahead) . . . no one ever asked me where I kept my feminine products. Think about it. We would get out of class early to change and ride the bus to an away game, sometimes an hour away. Then we would play a two to three hour game and drive all the way home. All done in our uniforms. Skin tight gray pants. It's not like I carried a purse.

Practices were the worst. We wore bright white pants, and the majority of the time was spent bent over the line of scrimmage in a three-point stance. One "accident" and I would NEVER have been able to step out onto the field with those boys again. They would have eaten me alive. Since no one has ever asked, I will keep the secret to myself. Let's just say I can be ingenious when necessary.

I vividly remember the trashy statements guys made in the presence of their peers, both about each other and females in our school. I wrote a short story in a creative writing college course about an episode which takes place between high school football players. The characters in the story talk about girls in a less-than-respectable way (to put it politely). It mirrored the types of conversations I heard amongst my team members almost daily (they became used to me eventually). The girls in my writing class stared at me with mouths agape, surprised the characters in my story would say such things. They shook their heads when they realized a girl had written the dialogue. The athletic guys in my class countered that it was very plausible. I had lived it.

Whatever you have seen in movies about guys dogging other guys and talking smack about girls, multiply it by a thousand, and that's about accurate. I remained silent on the periphery of the group, and most of the time, I didn't know who my teammates talked about anyway. They would goof around, wrestle, and be totally immature. It's not a stereotype, people, it's reality.

I ended up playing two years on the junior varsity team, and my second year as a junior, I played with all sophomores. Some of the guys had stronger, negative feelings about having a girl on their team. I found out later there was "talk" of trying to intentionally hurt me in practice, so I would be off the team. I proved the previous year that I clearly wasn't going anywhere. I'm not sure if it was just mentioned or if there was an actual plan in place. It might have been an untrue rumor. What I do know is there are good men in this world, too. One defended me.

Andy played tackle and stood next to me on the line. He was a humble, quiet sort but he was a strong guy. He wore flannel, drove a pickup truck, and probably really loved his mom, went to church, and owned a shotgun. He tucked his shirt in, which made him look like a lumberjack with wire rimmed glasses. He was smart but not an overachiever, a good football player but always in the background, and not cocky but confident.

Apparently, Andy stood up for me. I received the information second hand, but he told the thugs on the team something like, "if you hit her and she gets hurt accidentally, that's fine. But if you cheap shot her, you'll deal with me." Andy stood tall for me as a reminder of how people work unseen in the background of our lives and strive to ensure our success as comrades of whom we are completely unaware and who never ask for anything in return.

CHAPTER 7

THE END OF AN ERA

AFTER THE LAST HOME GAME of the season, we lined up on the sideline for our names to be called. A photograph of this moment during my first year still flashes in my memory. The entire team stood on the sideline looking up at the bleachers and a very petite me cried and waved at my mom with her camera. Coach moved down the line congratulating us individually. When he got to me, Coach Grosser gave me a hug and said, "Now that you're not my player, I can kiss you." And he gave me a fatherly kiss and told me he loved me. A couple years later he told me he loved me like a daughter (he had only sons), but if he had been my dad, he would never have let me play football. Fair enough. The end of season game during my second year was the same. When I graduated, Coach Grosser made a special effort and presented me with my diploma even though he wasn't one of the presenters.

So, this book was supposed to be about triathlons, right? Why write about a girl on the high school football team? Viking horns, white pants, special bathrooms . . . what does it all mean? My experience on the football team demonstrates how I dive into big things despite suffering palpitations and sweating episodes on a daily basis. I've always heard my own drumbeat, which I cannot help but follow. Sometimes, it would be easier to blend in, but I am glad I'm a unique person. We're all a bit strange on the inside, but, like I said before, some of us aren't afraid of it.

Fear pervades our culture, waits to hem us in, and keeps us from being bold in our lives. Fear is one of the devil's greatest tools used to keep us complacent, to hold us back from venturing to do great things.

I've always been stubborn, but this experience had me facing down fear every day. I had to look it in the eye and say, "I know you're there, but I'm coming anyway." I learned to *walk with fear, walk to fear, walk at fear.* I learned to *walk through fear.* I decided then I would not let fear rule my life or my decisions.

I'm not afraid of hard work, and I can persevere. I don't mind getting my hands dirty. I do what must be done to accomplish a goal. My brain and heart contain the mental stamina to endure, to continue, to strive even in unwelcoming and harsh conditions. I don't quit. I don't quit. I don't quit. I don't. I can't. I won't.

I love football. The sport is amazing and energizing and dynamic. I enjoy the strategy, the different positions, and the roles on offense and defense. I love the camaraderie, team building, and personal growth which happen on the field. I hold a special place in my heart for the stadium steps, the pre-game, and the competition. I adore the smell of the grass, the bleachers, and the yard line markers. To this day, I find tremendous peace sitting in an empty football stadium. I look back on my time on the team, and I smile from ear to ear. Would it have been more awesome if I was a better player? Maybe. But that's a hard sell. It was amazing. Hands down. I'd endure it all again to be able to play.

During my time on the team, a reporter contacted me once or twice asking for a story. I brushed them off, forcefully hanging up the phone. I never considered talking to them. A few times I imagined what the story would be like and how it would read. But realistically, I preferred that no one knew; I longed to avoid the spotlight.

A story about my time on the football team would have made me a target. An article would have distorted my intentions, which did not include the unwelcome by-product of notoriety. I just wanted to play football. I learned from the experience, and those lessons became embedded in the fabric of my existence, forever changing me and teaching me. My two seasons weren't about fame, they were about playing football.

If I could have played football as a girl without anyone knowing, I would have. Making it about my gender poisoned the experience and separated it from what it really was. Now, of course, playing football and being a girl could never be totally distinct, but I wanted to keep them as disconnected as I could while still being honest about both. During one of our dark, quiet, cement hallway pre-game sessions, Coach told the team I refused the interviews. I had mentioned it in passing. He thought it was a big deal.

When I trained for the Ironman, I wished I had Coach's address. Unfortunately, he retired and moved across the state. It would have been nice to let Coach Grosser know I'm still out there, doing it my way, pushing limits, and marching to my own drumbeat. In later years, I learned he passed away. To him and every other coach and player who struggled with this female football player invading their team, thank you from the bottom of my heart. Thank you for one of the greatest stories of my life. Thank you for the sacrifices you made on my behalf.

This experience also taught me a lot about humanity. People can be ugly. Sometimes they hurt or exploit others for their own gain. But, people can show up in immeasurable ways. Individuals like my cheerleader friend support us even when others do not. The Andys of the world stick up for what they feel is right (behind the scenes) with no expectation of acknowledgment. People, like Coach Grosser, impart the value of sportsmanship and teamwork despite the conditions or the odds. Parents love their children unconditionally and allow them to grow into the person God shapes them to be.

You see, God was in this. He worked in the people around me though I didn't see it at the time. With my head focused on the team, I missed God's performance. I've had a chance to reflect on my experience over the years. Today, I look for God in my everyday life and try to listen for His voice. When reminiscing about the story of my football days, I can't believe how spiritually deaf I was.

God ran with me on the field. He guided me and taught me to trust Him even in my difficult circumstances, to trust He works things together for my good. I had to lean on Him to get through every nail biting seventh period each day before practice (especially on split T drill days). He utilized the people in my life to prune me and my character. Playing football at Marysville High School served as a significant component of the foundation God laid for who He needed me to be.

CHAPTER 8

TO AND FRO

WHAT NEXT? HOCKEY? I WOULD love to tell you, dear reader, I went on to play hockey, but I can't really ice skate. When I skated for amusement in college, my skates slid into the grooves already on the ice, and I flailed out of control, following the path of a previous skater. Ha! Who gets stuck in the grooves on the ice?

My life has been interlaced with times of extreme regimen and diligence and periods of exceptional decadence and sloth-like abandon. I either go full bore or sit on the couch. In college, I fell off my regimental bandwagon and was a heap who studied. I ate a Wendy's single combo nearly every day. I wasn't obese, but I wasn't in shape. My skinny boyfriend and I weighed the same though he was 5'11," which was a kick in the teeth for me. A lightweight boyfriend seemed against the rules of nature, but what could I do? I smoked and drank and partied with everyone else. It was a time of fun and little responsibility as college often is. I graduated with a good degree from the University of Michigan. No harm, no foul.

Michigan had free workout facilities for the students. I went once, maybe twice in four years. Oh yes, I ran stadium steps one time, too. In the Big House. Nothing like picking the biggest stadium around to do steps. I made it a quarter of the way around only going sixty percent of the way up. I never made it back to the stadium to try a second time. I pounded a lot of steps that day for someone so out of shape. Time to hit Wendy's.

I wanted to get into graduate school for medicine, and I worked my tail off. My life was a lot of partying mixed in with studying and working; I paid for my college education and participated in work study. I desired to be fun and carefree but still wanted to be an "A" student. I felt humbled to go from being one of the best academically in my small high school and known for being "unique," to being ranked as "high mediocre" against my college peers and only a face in the crowd.

I struggled with who I was. While I attained some self-awareness in my early twenties, I didn't feel I had the license to be myself. After my high school experience, where I refused to back down from being me at any cost, I went into this time and place where I felt so lost.

I had an internal opposition raging within me (up until recently). On the one hand, I wanted to be the best, and I mean the *best*, at everything. I used this measuring rule for most of my life, which I failed to reach. I didn't need to be the best in the world, but I desired to be the best in the room. Was I the best at this activity within this group of people? I assessed the situation to evaluate whether I could compete with those surrounding me. On the other hand, I wanted people to like me. I craved for people to think highly of me, to value me, and to respect me. In my head, being liked and being the best went hand in hand.

In practice, this wasn't the case. People dislike those who continually compete with them and label them as overachievers. In high school, some students didn't relish my success, and, as a result, they didn't like me much. Occasionally, they responded with emotional hostility, though likely this was due to our immaturity. I struggled to be the best, and then felt sad when I wasn't liked. This inner skirmish continued through high school, into college, and through my early adult life. Unable to obtain balance, I felt "less than" or lonely.

I either felt "best" or "liked" but never both. I'm a very "black or white" person, which isn't necessarily bad. Some people are "waffly" and hesitant about everything to the point it's stifling. I'm the other extreme. The imbalance played itself out in my psyche manifesting as periods of extreme diligence and regimen mixed with times of stagnancy and lethargy. My early twenties were the latter.

After college, I moved to Chicago and worked at an insurance brokerage. I eventually found my way to a kickboxing studio and took classes. Within months, my life revolved around my kickboxing schedule. I attended classes, participated in weight training classes, used the heavy bags, ran with my training partners, and worked at the studio to pay for my classes. I spent 3-4 hours there a night, which was in addition to my regular full-time job. This focused schedule lasted for probably a year.

Eventually, I decided to go back to school and become a physician assistant. In undergrad, I wasn't aware the profession of physician assistant existed. In Chicago, my MCAT scores expired, and taking that test had been one of the worst experiences of my life. Even though I didn't have a personal relationship with God, I thought He had a plan for me. When a friend discussed applying to PA school, I thought graduate school might be a good path for me as well. I applied to two schools, and both institutions accepted me.

With school, my focus quickly shifted. Gone were the days of long workouts replaced by periods of smoking, drinking, and studying. My then boyfriend trained for a marathon, and I said, "Who would ever want to run that far?" I watched him run and applauded him, but we barely ever ran together. I hated running.

After I graduated from PA school, I moved to the Bronx, New York, to be part of a post-graduate training PA residency program in Obstetrics/Gynecology. We were workhorses. I didn't clock anywhere near the hours the residents did, but I plugged through twenty-eight-hour shifts when I was on call. I later worked in Gynecology Oncology at several hospitals and enjoyed living in New York. There were periods of hard work mixed with episodes of a more relaxed nature.

Though becoming a PA taxed my time and mind, I thrive in learning environments. It wasn't a stretch for me. Graduate school challenged me, but I wasn't out of my comfort zone. Getting my feet wet as a PA, however, was like being the "new guy" in a new position. It would take half an hour to find a culture tube and another thirty minutes to write a simple note on a patient. I had to get acclimated to the hospitals and the staff. I can come across as very harsh sometimes when I am focused, and I grappled with this from time to time. I still struggle with abrasive speech today.

I had trials in my twenties, but none were outside my wheel-house. Kickboxing was more time and schedule management as I never reached a competitive level. My biggest stress was, "Can I fit it all together and get the most out of the experience?" I learned planning organization, but I played it safe even then. I had competed on a guy's football team, so kickboxing in a co-ed class lacked the same monumental feeling.

During this period of complacency as a new PA, God sent me a wakeup call. He called me out of my box and challenged me with something totally unfathomable. Like with football, there were benefits I never could have foreseen. He changed my life forever.

PART TWO

THE PATH

CHAPTER 9

RUNNING CRAZY

IN 2006 I LIVED IN New York City, and my life was in a lull. My career cruised on autopilot. In my free time, I exercised three times a week with varying intensity, usually at the gym and usually for only 20 minutes. I loathed running because my chest felt like it could explode every time I tried. My friend, Cheryl, and I eked out 4.5 miles while running one day around the reservoir in Central Park, and this distance seemed like a colossal feat. We talked about how ridiculous running a marathon would be. Why run 26.2 miles? That's crazy. We both said one day we would like to run ten miles and decided this distance should be the golden number. Running made me feel like I was about to die. I tolerated the sweaty, head-pounding agony only to stay in shape and avoid weight gain. Painful or not, running is a great weight equalizer.

At this same time, I attended church on Sundays as a lukewarm Catholic. Because the Catholic Church seemed too male-centric, I spent several years away from any church in and after college. In Chicago I felt myself reaching for something more. A spiritual emptiness lurked inside me, and I found myself missing something though I didn't know what. I walked around my neighborhood one afternoon and stumbled upon a United Methodist Church, which I loved. Wendy was our pastor, and she was a great speaker. Somehow, she always seemed to speak directly to me, like she read my emails and had insider knowledge regarding the secret yearnings and questions of my heart.

After I moved from Chicago to New York, the only United Methodist churches I could find were in the ghetto, so I returned to the Catholic Church. I attended an uninteresting, monotone church in the Bronx, but then found a wonderful little church on the Upper East Side when I moved to Manhattan. The building was kitty-corner from my apartment with large columns and gobs of marble inside. Father Victor was such a character. He plowed through the Sunday night sermon in twenty-five minutes knowing most of the young people in attendance lacked abundant attention. When I felt prompted by the Spirit to confess my sins (though I didn't understand it was the Spirit at the time), I met with Father Victor and told him I needed to go to confession. The Catholic Church requires parishioners confess their sins to a priest. He said, "How long has it been since your last confession?"

"Maybe ten or twelve years," I replied.

He stopped and looked at me. "Well, why don't you just tell me one thing and then I'll absolve you." He loved efficiency. After saying my Hail Marys and Our Fathers for penance, I left the building. He was a good, humble man. Later, when I joined a Protestant church, I realized I could confess my sins directly to God, which forged a closer bond between me and the Lord.

One other time during the Easter Vigil mass, the church members were all outside, and Victor performed the blessing of the fire. While he prayed, the flames leapt up almost setting his robes and those of the altar server aflame. He stopped in the middle of the blessing and said, "Wow, we really got that going!"

The Catholics I know do not typically own Bibles, and I never was encouraged to read the holy book outside of church. Instead of providing Bibles for use during services, Catholic churches provide a smaller booklet of Bible readings and prayers in the pews. The booklet contains excerpts chosen by the Church or the Vatican or the Pope or somebody. Therefore, I lacked a good grasp of the Bible.

At this point in my life, I wrestled with whether I believed the Bible was authentic truth. Men penned the pages 2,000 years ago. How applicable could the message possibly be to me in modern times? I selected biblical passages from mass, which suited the life I wanted to lead, and latched onto those. I attended church regularly but disagreed with a lot of the Catholic Church doctrine.

But, it was more than that. I didn't know who God was and didn't understand why certain things in life happened. Doubt overcame me regarding religion. Even through my hesitation, I trusted God existed, however, I wasn't convinced Jesus was the son of God (my eyes fill with tears now as I write this).

God paved the way through the seeds of Wendy in the Methodist church and then with Father Victor in Manhattan, and I began a new relationship with God. Everything changed, though not abruptly. The heart transformation began subtly with shifts in rationale tiny enough for God to slide under my radar. He, being eternally wise, knew a frontal attack would be met with resistance. I'm stubborn, remember? Come at me with gloves up, and you'll get a fight.

It all began with a boy and a relationship (ain't that the truth) which went south in January of 2006. The breakup was terrible. The guy was totally wrong for me, but I really loved him and was devastated. In my post-break up depression, I called a different guy friend on the phone to get some clarity and a male perspective. He advised me to get out of my apartment. He said to make plans with people every night. On the evenings I was not hanging out with friends, I should hit the gym and work out until I passed out. This way I would not be sitting and waiting for the phone to ring and/or lying in bed awake trying desperately to fall asleep.

In stereotypical guy fashion, this friend does not remember telling me any of this. I, being in such a time of need, grabbed his advice with both hands. I began slowly, but eventually, I trolled the gym nightly, moving from the elliptical machine, to the Stairmaster, and to the weights for about one-and-a-half to two hours a pop. This pattern played out repeatedly for the next two months.

In April a guy from my book club asked me to go for a run, so we jogged in Central Park. He exhausted himself after three miles, but I felt great. The chest explosion resolved, I barely sweated, and I smiled the entire time. We ended our run, and I played it off like I was heading home, too. We parted ways and when he was out of sight, I ran again wondering how far I could go before I became tired. I ran three more miles. From my days of combating my depression at the gym, I was in excellent cardiovascular shape. I stopped after I ran six miles but knew I could have kept running. I was afraid to push myself too far too early given the possibility of an overrunning injury.

The next weekend I ran seven miles with shorter runs during the week. The weekend after that, I ran eight, and I progressed and increased my mileage. Eventually, I ploughed through long runs of fifteen miles. My legs would be sore after running, but overall, I experienced ease and a mental break from daily life. My first race was a half marathon in July of that year, which Cheryl had suggested after my running explosion began. She jumped on the running bandwagon as well and began increasing her distance. Both of us "why would anyone want to run more than 10 mile-ers" completed the 13.1-mile race, and I ran faster than I thought I could.

What did I love about running? The painful chest pressure and breathlessness experienced when someone initially starts running retreats as the new runner develops cardiovascular fitness, and calm and peace prevail. The mind is able to roam freely while the body functions like a machine whirring softly in the background. For me, though, it was more than this.

Running was freedom from my deepest anxiety. My relationship failure had confirmed my worst fear: I am unlovable. I have always had a low opinion of myself. I am highly critical of everything and suffer from self-loathing. My struggle for perfection and my super competitive spirit stem from a desire to be worthy of love. This pursuit caused me to inadvertently look for and attempt to correct every minute failure that existed in my life.

A "critic" always lived inside my brain. He spoke to me constantly saying things like, "you didn't say the right thing," "your outfit doesn't look as good as hers does," "look at you, you're fat," "you're stupid, "no one loves you," "you're not pretty at all," "your thighs are too fat," etc. He was there ALL the time. Sometimes it was unbearable. Most of the time, the voice sounded so familiar I didn't realize I was listening.

While out there on the roads running my little heart out in Central Park, I discovered the most amazing thing. I could outrun the critic. At some point during a long-distance run, the critic would get dropped. He couldn't keep up. The undertaking was no longer about form or technique or even speed. Fatigue would set in and, as I used all my energy to propel my body forward, he got shut down. This freedom was one of the huge draws of running for me. Freedom from my faults and sins! I could escape to a place of emotional and inner silence and safety where I didn't have to face the ever-commanding presence of my failure to be perfect. Out on the road I could be me, going forward at my own internal pace systematically moving through mile after mile. I was addicted to the changes in my body and the solace gained from running.

Other desirable benefits drew me to running as well. As it turns out, I'm a decent runner. I'm not a great runner, but in a race, I usually beat out seventy-five percent of the field. I am very performance driven, and, within a year, running became a new ruler, something to measure myself by. If I could run faster, then I would be better. Striving to be faster and be more competitive filled a need inside of me. *I may be fat, ugly, and unlovable, but I'm faster than you are, and I can prove it.* It was the proof I craved.

Running is definitive with set distances and documented speeds and progress. I needed that. Growing up I had academics to bolster me. *I may be fat, ugly, and unlovable, but I'm smarter than you are, and my exam grades prove it.* I never considered the possibility of the original thought being a lie. I wasn't fat, ugly, or unlovable. Michael J. Fox was quoted saying, "I am careful not to confuse excellence with perfection. Excellence, I can reach for; perfection is God's business."[1] This was a lesson I had yet to learn.

My feelings of low self-worth existed since childhood, but they blossomed in my twenties as I attempted to discover my identity. I had a hole inside of me. In high school, my identity was structured on academics and football. While as an adult in the workplace, I had neither of those. As God started to reveal His truth to me on my journey, I began to refer to the emptiness which existed inside of me as "the gap." For many years I tried to fill the gap with various things: relationships and physical intimacy with men, partying, getting good grades, perfectionism at work, and even competitive running. Though each of these things initially filled the gap, the wholeness was fleeting. This is why I returned to my routine gap fillers like an addict, trying to recreate feelings of wholeness. I strived to be perfect in my life in order to be "worthy," which never worked. Nothing worked. The gap was never permanently filled.

Apparently, I'm not the originator of the "gap" concept. People say we have a "God-sized space" inside of us we long to fill. We can attempt to fill it with other things, such as success, money, relationships, family, and addictions, which work for short periods of time. But eventually those things fail us, and then we are off looking for the next "fix." We seek the next thing to fill the gap in our hearts, sometimes without even realizing what we are doing. Individuals call it a God-sized gap because it is exactly that. God sized. I'm willing to bet people who, like me, tried to fill the gap with other things were only further disappointed after their short-term fixes did not pan out. I'll also wager people who learned to satisfy this gap with God have yet to be let down.

I began to realize a truth in my life. Only one thing ever made me feel I had enduring value. Two thousand years ago a man died on the cross for mankind, including me. Isaiah 53:5 reads, "But He *was* wounded for our transgressions, He *was* bruised for our iniquities; The chastisement for our peace *was* upon Him, And by His stripes we are healed" (NKJV). If Jesus is real, He died for me (not just for me but still for me). If Jesus is real and He died on the cross for my sins, then

I must be okay. I **MUST BE** worth something even if only something small. Prior to this, my life consisted of a wavering belief in Jesus, but now I seriously contemplated the gospel. Maybe Jesus was real. Maybe I had value apart from any race result, test score, or male interest. I mean, who willingly chooses to die for something worthless?

I do not remember exactly when, but I started to seek solace in Jesus. I read my Bible in small increments though most of it went over my head. I had purchased my Bible when my mom and I were bargain shopping, and I saw it on an aisle display table for $4.95. It was a good deal, and I thought to myself, *Maybe I'll need this one day.* That was years before I actually began studying its passages. As I read and my faith in Jesus solidified, I saw how my value has nothing to do with me and everything to do with God. In my life to date, Jesus is the only thing which filled the gap. He is the only thing that has never let me down.

CHAPTER 10
IRONMAN (NOT THE MOVIE)

I RAN IN A CIRCLE like a hamster, around and around in Central Park. I ran races and used my performances to define my innate worth, while a curiosity developed about Jesus. During this time, I studied my Bible frequently. Usually, I read for only five minutes, but I kept at it. I also became more involved with Father Victor's Catholic Church, for mostly selfish reasons. At work I gave patient case presentations which unnerved me, so I volunteered to be a lector (or reader) at church to help me get over my fear of public speaking. I also donated more money to church, though the amount was far from tithing. It felt good to give to God's Kingdom.

A girl who I met in a running club told me sometime in early 2007 that she was training for an Ironman. Little did I know how this piece of information would shape my life. An email I once received from *The Universe* (theuniverse@tut.com) stated, "For every physical adventure . . . there's the possibility of loss. That's what makes it an adventure. For every spiritual adventure, there's only gain. Which totally spoils the adventure, and is why you choose to forget that all physical adventures are really spiritual adventures."[2] Later, this would hit home. But when my friend first mentioned the race, I only had some vague notion. So, what exactly is an Ironman? I wondered . . .

To answer my own question, I spent time researching. I learned the race started in 1977 as an answer to the question: who are better athletes—swimmers, runners, or cyclists? A couple of groups in Hawaii picked a big swimming event, big cycling event, and the Honolulu marathon and put them together to see which group was the toughest.

The end result was a triathlon involving swimming 2.4 miles, biking 112 miles, and running 26.2 miles. The winner could call himself an Ironman. Now World Triathlon Corporation owns the phrase, and Ironman triathlons occur all over the world. The World Championships are held each year on the original course in Hawaii. 2.4-plus 112-plus 26.2 equals 140.6 miles.

Theodor Herzl said, "The body is a marvelous machine . . . a chemical laboratory, a power-house. Every movement, voluntary or involuntary, full of secrets and marvels!"[3] Moving 140.6 miles on an individual's own energy? That's a marvel all right.

When my friend divulged the race distance, I said aloud to her, "There's no way I could ever do that." And then I felt this sudden twinge in my left side flank; I may have even looked over my shoulder wondering what it was. In a later instance, I chatted with nurses at work about this particular friend, and I again said, "Oh, I could never do that" and felt the twinge again. Somewhere inside me, I heard a voice. The Holy Spirit (though I didn't know it at the time) said, "Because you don't want to or because you don't think you can?"

Here is where my imagination runs amok. When I look back and ponder this moment in my life, I imagine God sitting at His desk in His office in heaven. Jesus kneels on the floor next to an open filing cabinet drawer humbly doing some filing. God slams His fist down on His desk and mutters, "Man, oh, man, when is this child going to get it? That all things are possible through Me? Wasn't football enough?" Jesus looks at His Father calmly, gently shrugs His shoulders, and resumes His quiet filing. God's fist remains clenched. "Well, Jesus, We're about to school this one."

I will never be sure if that's how it went down, but the twinge I felt when discussing the Ironman never left me. I felt it over and over again. I continued hearing the voice of the Holy Spirit inside me question, "because you don't want to or because you don't think you can?" It nagged and nagged, cropping up in my thoughts all the time. At one point I prayed, *Please, let this feeling leave me alone. The race is too far, and it would take too much to try.* My prayer went unanswered or more likely God answered with a silent, "No."

Finally, I relented. In my inner recesses I resolved I would attempt an Ironman triathlon. I submitted to the never-ending "twinge" and agreed to try my hand at the race. I shared this with no one because of the high probability of an epic fail.

In an email devotional from *Proverbs 31 Ministries,* Wendy Pope wrote, "Have you ever said "yes" to God for what you believed was the assignment of a lifetime? When you said "yes" did you know you would never be the same again?"[4] I was about to learn.

Romans 8:28 says, "And we know that all things work together for the good of those who love God, to those who are the called according to His purpose" (NKJV). This statement rings true even when we cannot see that purpose. *Especially* if we cannot see the purpose. I felt called to a triathlon, and the calling I sensed was undeniable. The goal ahead overwhelmed me. In truth I needed a Savior, but I wasn't astute enough to know I needed a Savior. I thought I needed a plan. So, plan, I did.

I decided on an order of events. My 2007 New Year's Resolution had been to complete my first marathon. I built on this resolution: first marathon 2007, first triathlon 2008, and first Ironman 2009. Epictetus noted, "First say to yourself what you would be; and then do what you have to do." Easy enough, right? I had enough time to train to get there. What could go wrong? Well, a small glitch existed in my plan: I didn't know how to swim.

In high school we had to pass a 100-yard swim test in order to graduate. I took swim lessons as a small child and could jump in a pool without drowning, but that was the extent of my swimming capabilities. One hundred yards seemed an extraordinary length when my maximum swim distance was just over to the side wall. Placing my face in the water while trying to freestyle during the swim test as a 17-year-old felt very disconcerting, and I experienced panic and anxiety. I suffered an asthma attack (I have a history of asthma) and had to get out of the water. I went into the locker room and to calm down and use my inhaler. I eventually felt well enough to retry the test and barely passed. I kept my face above water this time and went slowly. Having my face in the water terrified me. Every time I tried, I felt like I was drowning.

Fast forward from the high school pool to New York City fifteen years later. I had just dedicated myself to training regularly and attempting an Ironman with a swim distance of 2.4 miles, yet I needed a Valium and resuscitation every time I tried to swim ten yards. God works counterintuitively. Jesus came in the form of a helpless baby born in a stable and not warring as a glorious king. God presents Himself to us in ways we could never predict in a million years.

Charles Swindoll has daily devotional called *Bedside Blessings,* and I received it at a women's retreat through my friend's church. My favorite entry is as follows:

> "God is not known for doing standard things. He is engaged in doing very distinct things. When a person does something, it has the man or woman look about it. It drips with humanity. You can follow the logic of it and see the meaning behind it. You can even read what they paid for it and how they pulled it off and the organization that made it so slick. God doesn't build skyscrapers; men build skyscrapers. And they all have the touch of genius, human genius. But you cannot find a man who can make a star. And when God steps in, His working is like the difference between a skyscraper and a star."[5]

The Bible says, "'For my thoughts are not your thoughts, neither are your ways my ways,' declares the Lord" (Isaiah 55:8, NIV). The quote and verse above strike a chord in my heart about the unfathomable nature of God's plan. I never imagined an Ironman would be the way He'd reach out to me. God positioned me to be an endurance triathlete, where I would have extensive time alone on the road to spend with Him.

The thought of swimming sent shivers down my back. Two miles of freestyle in a lake? It might as well have been across the Atlantic because I couldn't swim one lap in a pool. My heart pounded, palms sweated, my mind raced, my breathing quickened, and I stifled the overwhelming urge to run away when I thought of the two-mile swim. Fear knocked at my door, or better yet, tried to beat the door down. But, learning to swim was impossible to avoid.

"The best way out is always through" says Robert Frost[6], and I lived this truth on the football field. The quickest way to overcome fear is to run directly at it, shortening the time panic has control. If I hide from my trepidation, fear will find me at another time and place, growling and baring its ugly teeth.

A human tendency exists to believe the "other guy" has it all together, and we alone struggle. This isn't true. Everyone wrestles with issues daily. Mark Twain notes, "Courage is resistance to fear, mastery of fear—not absence of fear."[7] All people feel fear; some just don't let it stop them.

I had to start somewhere with swimming, and I opted for lessons. I signed up for beginning swim classes at the Y near my apartment in NYC. The swim sessions challenged me both psychologically and physically. A triathlete can muscle their way through biking and running, but swimming is based on technique. My first lesson demoralized me. I could barely make it down one length of the pool. Each time I reached the end of the lane, I grabbed ahold of the wall, hauled my chest up on the side, and gasped as if I'd just been strangled for several minutes. This sensation persisted for a grueling three to four months. I would swim one or two lengths, rest at the wall, and chat with the lifeguard for several minutes. Each length was twenty-five yards. An Ironman swim is 4,224 yards. *Gulp.*

Not being able to swim fifty yards without needing CPR while simultaneously completing long marathon training runs of fifteen-plus miles frustrated and humiliated me. I befriended a couple of the fast swimmers in the lane next to me over the course of several weeks.

The girls at the pool, Maggie and Allie, sympathized and encouraged me. To watch them effortlessly plow through the water humbled me as I floundered. Being fast wasn't even something I dared to hope for. Instead, I wished to be a steady, even swimmer. Forget the 4,224 yards. I set my sites on a 1,000-yard continuous swim.

My Ironman friend, who was in recovery mode after her race, said she swam for twenty-five minutes. Feeling disheartened, I said, "That's so great. I could never swim for twenty-five minutes straight."

"Sure, you could," she said, "maybe not fast but you could." I waved the thought away in my mind, and she challenged me. "Go and force yourself to swim for twenty-five minutes without stopping." I accepted her challenge, and wouldn't you know it, I swam twenty-five minutes straight! I wondered how much I've let my own mind limit me.

CHAPTER 11

THE COMFORT ZONE

"Immediately Jesus made the disciples get into the boat and go on ahead of him to the other side, while he dismissed the crowd. After he had dismissed them, he went up on a mountainside by himself to pray. Later that night, he was there alone, and the boat was already a considerable distance from land, buffeted by the waves because the wind was against it.

Shortly before dawn Jesus went out to them, walking on the lake. When the disciples saw him walking on the lake, they were terrified. 'It's a ghost,' they said, and cried out in fear.

But Jesus immediately said to them: 'Take courage! It is I. Don't be afraid.'

'Lord, if it's you,' Peter replied, 'tell me to come to you on the water.'

'Come,' he said.

Then Peter got down out of the boat, walked on the water and came toward Jesus. But when he saw the wind, he was afraid and, beginning to sink, cried out, 'Lord, save me!'

Immediately Jesus reached out his hand and caught him. 'You of little faith,' he said, 'why did you doubt?'"

This story from Matthew 14:22-31 (NIV), about Peter confused me as a child. Jesus told him to have courage. Why wouldn't Peter keep walking? Why would he doubt? It made no sense. "I can do all this through him who gives me strength" (Philippians 4:13, NIV). Right? Why the difficulty? A glaring difference exists between knowing a truth and living it, between reading something in a book and walking it out. To stand at the back of our comfort zones and *say* we have faith is different than teetering on the edge of the abyss of what we know (toes hanging over) and *acting out* our faith.

Let's step away from the story for a bit. What exactly am I talking about? Everyone has a comfort zone where they feel safe. Imagine a piece of string extending across your living room floor. The piece of string represents the edge of the comfort zone of your life. One side of the room is familiar and filled with light, and darkness shrouds the other side of the wholly unknown. Growth occurs at the periphery of the light when we toe the line with the unknown. When we prepare to take a step into unknown territory, we must trust God. While in the light, we stand on familiar ground, relying on own steps and strength. We step to the line when we face something bigger than ourselves. When we relax in the back of our comfort zones, we take no risks and remain complacent. Do nothing, gain nothing. Stagnancy.

For me, athletics fall outside my comfort zone. People tend to think I'm a natural athlete. I'm not. I am in the minority of people who were in much better shape at the age of thirty-five (training for an Ironman) than they were at the age of sixteen. In high school, I rode the bench most of the time and not only in football.

A solid work ethic is my gift. When it comes to elbow grease, I max out. I broke through the odds to play football and endured physically demanding practices. I gutted through the first three to four months of swim training. I can handle grueling; I know because I lived it. I do not shy away from difficult tasks, and I'm unafraid to test myself. I don't quit, I don't quit, I don't quit. Put the yoke on me, and, no matter what the weather, the field will get plowed. God blessed me with gumption.

People ask me how I stay motivated. I have no idea. I've never had to seek motivation. At baseline, I am absolutely relentless. I listened to *Uncommon* by Tony Dungy in my car, and he says, "Failure doesn't mean it's final."[8] Furthermore, Mary Pickford says, "If you have made mistakes, even serious ones, there is always another chance for you. What we call failure is not the falling down but the staying down."[9] I truly believe that. Failure isn't a dead end but an intersection to be negotiated. It's not over until we stop trying to get it right.

This is the reason I hedged when I felt God's call to the Ironman race. If I set out to do this, I would show up at the start line of an Ironman. The race would be tough and require hours upon hours of preparation and sacrifice. If I committed to the race, I would be compelled to complete the training. In *I Ain't Never Been Nothing but a Winner*, author Paul "Bear" Bryant writes, "It's not the will to win that matters . . . everyone has that. It's the will to prepare to win that matters."[10]

Now, let's go back to the string on the floor which divided the room into your comfort zone and the unknown. Why do we get stuck in complacency if growth occurs at the edge of the string as we venture into the unfamiliar? Are we opposed to growth? No, fear and pain reside outside of our comfort zones. The enemy waits to battle us in the unfamiliar darkness. Growth of any kind, whether it be spiritual, intellectual, or physical, transpires when we step out of our comfort zone and try what is beyond our limits.

Like Peter in the verses at the beginning of the chapter, it's easy to doubt, to be afraid of what we do not know. It's convenient to stay in the boat, surrounded by safety and familiarity. Peter had courage to get out and try, but he faltered when he saw his circumstances.

Isaiah 41:10 gave me great comfort during my training. "So do not fear, for I am with you; do not be dismayed, for I am your God. I will strengthen you and help you; I will uphold you with my righteous right hand" (NIV). God invites us to grow with Him, go with Him, and be molded by Him. He knows we will encounter fear, which is why He reassures us to not be afraid. He will strengthen us. He will uphold us. He guarantees it. The God of Truth promises to be there through our trials and in our growth as we step over the string.

The Ironman was my string. The race was a bigger undertaking than I could achieve by myself. I accepted in the beginning that God bringing me on the journey didn't necessarily mean He wanted me to complete the race. Finishing seemed like such a long shot. I needed God's assistance because I lacked the physical ability to conquer this on my own. It took something as big as training for an Ironman for me to reach out my hand to God for help. Once I did, I realized He had always been holding it. God called me out of the boat with the Ironman.

CHAPTER 12

STEP ONE

I RAN THE CHICAGO MARATHON in October 2007. Someone in my running club participated in Chicago a few years prior, and the weather topped out at thirty-seven degrees. The day I geared up to run, the sun blazed in at eighty-seven degrees. The race organizers were unprepared and didn't have enough water at the aid stations. Later, I learned that five people had died. Ultimately, authorities canceled the race and hauled runners off the course. I managed to make it ahead of the cutoff and was allowed to run across the finish line. The heat and dehydration wreaked havoc on me as I vomited what seemed to be liters of putrid Gatorade that had fermented in my stomach. However, I completed step one: I was a marathoner.

During the fall of 2007, my involvement in my faith grew. Father Victor waved and smiled at me when he saw me. I became a regular lector at the Sunday night service. After church each week, I walked up to the six-foot-tall statue of Jesus in the front right corner of the altar. I knelt, cried, and prayed. For the longest time, I couldn't bring myself to touch the stone-carved Jesus because I did not feel worthy enough to do so.

Over time as the gift of God's grace became reality, I began to place my hand on his feet and look up into his lifelike face as I cried and prayed. My heart stirred every time. Finally, after months, feeling the love He had for me, I held his outstretched hand. The depression, feelings of unworthiness, shame, and guilt poured out of me as I surrendered at the foot of Christ in a very literal sense.

Do we need statues to look into the face of Jesus? No. We can pray to Jesus right where we sit now. God utilized this physical representation because that's what I needed at the time in order to see Him. My faith developed, I learned how to pray, and God used Father Victor's church to accomplish His purpose.

I endeavored to read my Bible daily and kept it on my bedside table. Some weeks I was more successful than others, but I plodded along reading a paragraph or two every day. I suppose having the holy book in my bedroom served as a reminder for me to make better choices with men.

The Catholic Church offers an observance called Veneration of the Cross during Good Friday services. I still love the Catholic Church Good Friday mass. In New York City, we gathered in the streets and ambled the distance Jesus walked from Jerusalem to Calvary where the authorities crucified Him. Someone in front of the march carried a large cross and throngs of people sang hymns as we solemnly walked. Hundreds and hundreds of people marched in the police cordoned streets.

Once the walk was over, our church members congregated at our church for service. We read the Passion of Christ after which Veneration of the Cross began. The priest held a cross in front of the altar, and the entire Parrish stood in line to pay our respects to our Savior and His sacrifice. Churchgoers could touch or kiss the cross. Father Victor advised us to lay our failures (and our successes) at the foot of the cross when it was our turn. I found closeness to God and experienced weightlessness by releasing my past hurts to Jesus. I practiced my own Veneration of the Cross by kneeling at the altar each week before my pilgrimage to the Jesus statue.

God first spoke to me in Father Victor's church. It wasn't a booming voice in the rafters or a burning bush in the aisle, but it was Him. I stood listening to Father Victor read the Gospel of John as I followed along in the missalette (booklet), which contains the weekly Bible passages (Catholics read the same verses whether in Michigan or Italy).

He came to verse 15:16a. The words leapt off the page when I read them and as they were spoken aloud. It was as if a gong had been struck in my heart and I could feel the reverberations. **"You did not choose me but I chose you. And I appointed you to go and bear fruit, fruit that will last"** (NRSVCE). I couldn't take my eyes off the verse. I read and re-read it over and over again. God emblazoned the words in my mind. During the sermon, I kept looking down at the missalette open in my lap, reading and re-reading the verse. When I went to mass for the next couple of weeks, I repeatedly turned back to this passage from John. I re-read this verse again and again.

One week, I realized we would soon progress to new missalettes as they changed with each season of the church. I quickly flipped back and memorized the verse number. I wrote it down in my Bible when I got home. I couldn't bear not knowing where to find these words. It was a lifeline.

I meditated on and pondered this verse for a long time. *What did He mean, "I chose you"? What did He choose me for? Could I be worth choosing?* He was telling me, "Whatever your flaws are, I choose you. You are Mine. You are called." I didn't know what He chose me for, but emotion flooded me like water over a breaking dam, and I started listening for God.

Now I'm not implying I'm the "chosen one" or the Messiah or something. God desires a personal relationship with each of us. He died for every single person ever created. Sadly, not everyone accepts His sacrifice. Through this verse, God showed me the gift of His grace. He didn't base my forgiveness on my performance, my abilities, or my failures. He chose me and forgave me because of who He is.

When I began the journey toward the Ironman, I realized I was ready to leave New York City. I treasured my time in the hustle and bustle, the culture, the plethora of restaurants, and the opportunities for unique experiences. But, New York is pagan and materialistic on many levels, and my focus in life rapidly changed. I moved from the

Manolo Blahnik/Tiffany phase of my life to the Salvation Army phase. I cared less about what I had and more about who I was.

I decided training for an Ironman required more room, more open roads. New York City is crowded. I enjoyed riding in New Jersey over the George Washington Bridge with the panoramic views of the city but cycling from my apartment to the GW put my life in the hands of city taxi drivers. It was time for a change of venue.

CHAPTER 13

THE NEXT MOVE

A FRIEND FROM CHARLOTTE, NORTH Carolina, encouraged me to join her, enticing me with the blue sky and warmer climate. The flight time from Charlotte equaled that of New York, so distance from my family wasn't a consideration. I flew to Michigan from New York for the Wolverines' first home football game of the season against Appalachian State, which I found out is in North Carolina. As I boarded the plane, I offered a pseudo-discernment-prayer, *Okay God, if Appalachian State beats Michigan, I will consider it a sign I'm supposed to move to North Carolina.* The game resulted in Michigan's most famous loss on record. Needless to say, I do not pray things like that anymore. *Men may come and go, but your football team is forever. Go Blue!*

I interviewed in Charlotte and took a job in pain management because the location and hours were best for training. I relocated in March 2008 and started training for the NYC triathlon two days after arriving. I picked a sprint triathlon in June for my first triathlon and a race back in New York City as my second stepping stone toward my goal of becoming a triathlete. The NYC triathlon was my "A-race" or my "big goal" of the season. A coworker, Alison, was a triathlete as well and had swum on the UCLA water polo team in college.

I met Alison when I interviewed for the pain management physician group; she also was employed by the practice. She is an example of what it means to love Jesus and now lives in Africa as a missionary. Al welcomed me into her group of Christian friends, who remain some of the best people I know. They continue to be my accountability partners, my prayer warriors, and my cheerleaders. Each of them nurtures a strong relationship with Jesus. They showed me what a woman walking with Christ looked like. God puts the right people in our lives at exactly the right time.

I met a "Christian" man during this time. He was Baptist and introduced me to church outside of the Catholic mass I usually attended, which was a huge step for me. I never considered a Baptist church prior to our relationship. He encouraged me to read the Bible, which we would do together, and he purported to follow God's laws and principles.

After a time though, it became clear he lacked obedience to many of the principles he taught me. He had a woman living at his house and lied to me about it. He was untruthful about his finances which I found out when the bank foreclosed on his house. He evaded questions about past relationships, and he had two children he never mentioned. Genesis 50:20 says, "You intended to harm me, but God intended it for good to accomplish what is now being done, the saving of many lives" (NIV). Whatever his faults, this relationship led me to step outside the Catholic faith. God used my ex-boyfriend for good in my life, and my personal relationship with God's Word deepened.

While still in this relationship, I prepared for my first triathlon event. Alison advised me to begin open water swimming. I slogged my way through the pool and could swim the 800m for the sprint triathlon, though not with any speed or form. However, the swim took place in a lake, which is very different from swimming in a pool. For starters, the particles in the water decrease visibility, and lack of lane lines makes swimming straight a challenge. I trained myself to look up every ten to twelve strokes and "sight" to establish the correct direction.

I went for my first open water swim practice in Lake Norman near Charlotte. As I stood at the edge of the water hyperventilating with the feeling of panic gripping my chest, I tried to breathe deeply to calm myself. I overheard a Team-in-Training coach encourage his athletes. His advice was God-sent.

"So how far do you have to swim?" he questioned the would-be swimmers.

"To the next buoy," they replied in unison.

"That's right," he said. "No matter how far the swim is, no matter how far until the finish line, you only have to swim to the next buoy. Once you get there, then you only have to swim to the *next* buoy. But to the next buoy is as far as you ever have to go!"

I slyly tried to inch closer to ensure I was privy to the entire conversation. I lived by those words of wisdom and encouragement. *I only have to get to the next buoy*, I thought to myself, *I can manage that.*

We lined up in the water. When the whistle blew, I waited for everyone else to start so I wouldn't be thrashed by other swimmers. Images of drowning victims danced through my mind and my heart pounded in my chest. Unfortunately, it was like the high school swim test all over again. I couldn't breathe or swim. The claustrophobia from the inability to see in the water gripped me, and I lifted my head gasping with each stroke. I flailed for the first 300 yards. I settled into a frog-like-pseudo-breaststroke with my head above water until I felt like I wanted to try freestyle again. My heart rate must have been 250 beats per minute. I kept at it, and things leveled out some. I made it through the practice swim without drowning or quitting. These panic attacks repeated themselves every time I attempted swimming in the open water.

My spiritual transformation continued. I went to a sermon at Mecklenburg Community Church with Alison in July 2008 that changed my life. Pastor James White based his message entitled "Taking Down the High Places" on the book of Kings. He recounted how we, as Christians, typically hold five percent of ourselves back from God. We give our lives to God but refuse to relinquish *just a little bit* of the bad habits and pleasurable things of our past. Sex was one of those things for me.

Prior to the sermon, marrying someone without having a prior physical relationship seemed ridiculous. To commit my entire life to someone without having knowledge of their whole being was a recipe for failure. It occurred to me after hearing this sermon that the point is to trust God will pick someone who is right for me, someone who will fit with me completely. The sad reality is I tried it my way for years without getting anywhere. Men repeatedly hurt me and took advantage. I cannot blame them; I did not value myself either.

I thought and toiled over this. God called me to give up the emotional pain of seeking human intimacy as a form of acceptance and to trust His judgment rather than my own. I had no idea how I would ever survive celibacy with the pressures of society and our culture bearing down on me. I lost my virginity as a teenager and could not undo my past actions. I had experienced sexual intimacy with men and enjoyed it. Choosing to follow God's command of no sex before marriage was one of the most difficult decisions I ever made. But God's Word is not ambivalent on this matter. God makes it clear His best for me is a sexual relationship inside of a marital commitment. I pledged to refrain from sex until I married.

As I exhaled after making the decision, my whole body felt lighter. I agonized over this choice but once I surrendered this area of my life to God, the strain of it eased. Matthew 11:28-30 reveals, "Come to me, all you who are weary and burdened, and I will give you rest. Take my yoke upon you and learn for me, for I am gentle and humble in heart, and you will find rest for your souls. For my yoke is easy and my burden is light" (NIV).

God is our Father, and we stumble like toddlers learning to walk. He stands with arms outstretched waiting to catch us when we fall. We have only to let go and try. And what happens when a small child takes their first steps? The father picks them up into his arms with hugs and kisses and celebrates the first wobbly steps with cheering and affirmation. Our heavenly Father affirms us in the same way. God waits for us to release what holds us back from Him. His arms are right there, outstretched, guiding us, protecting us, and encouraging us.

Making the choice to obey God's edicts plagued me as I imagined scenarios of rejection, loneliness, and gut-wrenching temptation. Sex is everywhere in our culture. However, when I let go of my own burden, God put peace in my soul, peace from trying to impress men with my body.

I was full of hope that I had a greater worth than being just a sexual object. Martha Graham says, "The body is a sacred garment."[11] God Himself tells us the same thing in His Word. Romans 12:1-2 reads, "I beseech you therefore, brethren, by the mercies of God, that ye present your bodies a living sacrifice, holy, acceptable unto God, which is your reasonable service. And be not conformed to this world: but be ye transformed by the renewing of your mind, that ye may prove what is that good, and acceptable, and perfect, will of God" (KJV).

My physical being was sacred; it wasn't meant to be given away carelessly without deep consideration. God designed my body to honor Him. I released the untruth that I needed to have sex to be feminine and powerful and desirable.

Have I been perfect? No, I test the waters seeing how far I can go until I feel guilt creep in. I broke my promise several times; I'm not perfect. Sex acts as a catalyst and propels us into a deep emotional connection before solid intellectual and spiritual foundations are in place. The imbalance tips the scales causing fights, promoting unrealistic expectations, and blurring our vision of the other person's true character. Do I miss sex? Sure, I do. I am human and crave intimacy. But I feel protected, safe, and loved when I stick to my commitment in ways I never could before. I trust that God *always* has my best in mind. I have never met a person about whom I could say the same.

Dating with an ideal of purity has not been easy. Nowhere in the Bible is it written that following God is easy. Men rejected me because I won't sleep with them. Several unbelieving friends stopped talking to me because I changed this practice in my life. A non-Christian even told me I will likely never marry as a result. Every time I start to question whether I made the right decision, God sends affirmation my way in the form of a personal encounter, a text, or a social media post to let me know He still has my back.

CHAPTER 14

STEP TWO

THE DAY OF MY SPRINT triathlon arrived. The start air horn was set to blast at 6:30 a.m., and I pulled into the parking area around 4:30 a.m. Fear can function as an early wake up call. I walked along the dark, quiet road after I locked my car. I carried my race equipment and walked my bike. As I rounded the last corner, the bright lights and humming sound of a generator accosted me. I have come to know and love this sound as part of the great ritual that is race day morning. Triathlons frequently occur in outlying areas and start at the crack of dawn, so generators and portable lights are a mainstay. Electric energy ricocheted amongst the participants as athletes grabbed their gear and bikes before the race.

Each age group wears the same color swim cap, so athletes have a visual on their age range competitors while in the water. Instantly, I felt camaraderie with those walking the plank with me after race organizers summoned our group to the start corral. My face contorted, and I focused on the blades of grass underneath my bare feet as I struggled not to cry. The swim petrified me. As my age category waded out into the water, I stuck to the back rationalizing it was advantageous to let the good swimmers go first rather than have them swim over me.

The horn sounded. I perceived a few crowd cheers, but the sound of splashing water predominated as the athletes initiated their frantic stroking and arm rotations. I paddled reasonably well for the first few strokes, but then panic ensued all over again. I swam my frog-like-breast-stroke for about fifty percent of the time to the first buoy.

I just have to get to the first buoy, I thought to myself.

Slowly, I made my way one yellow buoy by one yellow buoy. The distance to the turnaround point seemed much farther than it should be. At one point, I swam off course and one of the kayak lifeguards whistled me back. I inadvertently paddled farther than the required distance (*great*). I worked to improve my sighting.

Finally, I reached the orange buoy, which signaled the turn back to the beach. I glanced back, and the next few waves of swimmers (in their different colored swim caps) were seconds behind. Eating the dust of people who started three, six, and nine minutes after I did, humbled me.

Just keep going.

I progressed from buoy to buoy. Once, on my way back to shore, I caught myself swimming on the wrong side of the buoys, going against other swimmers. I righted myself and continued to try to sight better. Eventually, I saw the shore clearly, and I struggled my way in. Finally (*thank You, Jesus!*), I stood and slightly stumbled through the sand and then up the grassy hill to the paved parking lot where my bike, Lucy, waited.

Now, a lot of people name their bikes and a lot of people don't. I named my bike because God sent her to assist me in my journey. While living in New York City, I prayed for the right bicycle for two or three months. On my way to one of my part time jobs in the Bronx, the city bus I rode drove right past a bicycle shop. One day when I got off work, I noticed they were still open. I went in expectantly feeling this was where I would find my bike. I had looked in multiple other stores, but the Manhattan bike shop guys seemed too much like used car salesman with their slick talk.

I surveyed the bikes and knew she was mine the second the shop owner showed her to me. The frame was painted simple black and gray, but she felt like my bike. I test rode her on a trainer and confirmed my initial sentiment. I selected the cheapest shoes they had, bike pump, helmet, bike shorts, and some other little things. My budget for the bike was $1100, which was the exact price on the tag. However, with all the extras, the cost was over budget at $1360. I strictly adhere to my budget to avoid racking up debt. I pay my credit card balance every month. If I don't have enough money to pay the balance every billing cycle, then I shouldn't be buying things.

I pondered what to do next though I felt sure I was supposed to purchase the bike. I told the owner I would pay him half of the cost that day and would return to pay for the rest and pick up the bike once I figured out where in the budget I could pull the money from. The store was underneath the subway tracks, and I exited the store. I walked a few paces when my phone signaled I had a voicemail. I hadn't gotten the call while in the store since my phone had no reception. The message was from my boss at my part time job asking if I could pick up some extra work. Someone had signed up to work and now was unable to fulfill their commitment.

Do you know how much I got paid for this? It was almost to the dollar exactly what I was short. Lucy was meant to be my bike. I prayed for her and God provided for her completely.

I remembered this story as I trotted amongst the bike racks and saw her hanging in my spot. My Lucy. I averaged 17mph during the bike segment, and my run was strong. I competed on the novice day whereas most of the seasoned triathletes raced the day before. I came in nineteenth overall in the women's category. My run split was seventh overall, my bike split was sixth overall, and my swim split was one hundred seventeenth overall. Swimming was clearly the most difficult of the three for me. But it didn't matter; I finished. New Year's Resolution #2: become a triathlete . . . *check*.

I raced the sprint triathlon to get my feet wet. My "A-race" of the year was the NYC triathlon in New York. The sprint had an 800m swim, 17-mile bike, and a 3.1-mile run. NYC was an Olympic or International distance which included a 1500m swim, a 25-mile bike, and a 6.2-mile run. I headed back to my old digs to race around the boroughs and swim in the Hudson River. Yes, I said it, swim in the Hudson River. *(Yuck. That river is so full of muck.)*

This race had a few big upsides. I volunteered the year before and knew the course and the transition area layouts. I also had friends to stay with and cheer for me. Most of all, the Hudson River boasts a very fast current, which would work in my favor. Now we're talking.

I geared my training program for this distance from the get go and had thrown the sprint race into the schedule as a practice run. I slogged away in the pool for seventy-seven minutes during my longest swim workout before NYC. I am not sure how many yards I swam as my training program was organized in minutes. This was before I learned to drill or swim sets, so I mindlessly swam back and forth with a terribly inefficient stroke for minutes upon minutes.

I remember getting up at 4:30 a.m. for early morning bike rides. The black globs of old gum refracted like glass in the illumination from my headlamp, and the lack of light slowed my speed. The world was so calm and cool that early in the morning. Businesses were closed, people were sleeping, and the peace was unbroken by the sounds of cars.

It wasn't all fun. Getting up at oh-dark-thirty was hideous at times. I exercised without caffeine and fatigue weighed me down like a wet blanket. Plus, by the time I finished my ride at 6:00 a.m. or 6:30 a.m., the rest of the world was now driving to work and in a rush. The tension as I rode home contrasted the peace I felt as I rode out.

By the end of my training plan, I felt ready for the NYC race. The biggest logistical issue prior to the competition was getting Lucy to the Big Apple on an airplane. A bike mechanic broke her down into several pieces and tucked her in a bike suitcase I rented. I struggled with the unwieldy box as the weight wasn't evenly distributed. I smiled from ear to ear when I retrieved her from the baggage guy upon my arrival in the city. I took the shuttle from JFK to Grand Central, and the driver helped me with the bulky bike box. After the bus, I took a cab to my friend's apartment. The taxi driver began repeatedly slamming the trunk lid down to get the bike suitcase to fit.

"Whoa! That's my bike. Be careful! If you hurt my bike, we are going to have a serious problem here." Very serious. He gave me a look and slammed the trunk.

I stayed with my friend, Joey. She trucked along with me to a bike shop to have Lucy reassembled. I observed him reconstruct my baby, so I could reassemble her at home. Once she was together, I wheeled Lucy a mile down the sidewalk to Joey's apartment along with the giant bike box. The following day, race day eve, I rode my bike over to the race transition area and left her there with the security guards as per the race day guidelines.

Joey awoke with me on race day morning at 3:30 a.m. in order to make it to the transition area (TA for short) by 4:30 a.m. We caught a cab and zipped over. Triathletes keep their race gear in the TA. Running, biking, and swimming require a lot of stuff, and athletes need an organized place to put everything. Racks for bikes line the TA because no self-respecting cyclist has a kickstand (the equivalent of a pocket protector in cycling). Riders hook their bikes on the rack by the seat or the handlebars, and the small space underneath the bike forms the racer's transition area. Usually, I set out a towel along with the different shoes, sunglasses, and hats I will need to change from one discipline to the next.

We arrived, and the electric feeling in the morning darkness with the lights shining overhead and the generators humming greeted us. People milled around like busy ants, and the bikes shone with all their bright colors glinting in the artificial light. *(Holy cow, I am about to jump into the Hudson River. God help me.)*

I placed my race items on the towel under my bike, and a volunteer body-marked me (a triathlon term meaning: wrote my race number on my arms with a Sharpie marker). I put on my wetsuit (you didn't think I swam in the Hudson River in just a bathing suit, did you?). Getting into a wetsuit is a lot like putting on rubber skin. I slathered Body Glide on my joints and neck to help with chafing and then slowly, inch by inch, peeled the rubber up my body to make sure it was smooth because wrinkles increase surface drag in the water. I had practiced swimming with my wetsuit on a couple times in the pool, which earned me some weird looks at the gym. I improved my donning skills over time, but it was a huge hassle back then.

Finally, I walked the mile down to the swim start (*who planned these logistics?*). People swarmed the sidewalk, and the jaunt took longer than I prepared for. People thronged the timing chip distribution area like bugs on an anthill. This timing chip is registered to your number and documents your splits (swimming/biking/running times) as you run over mats at various locations. I put my chip on a strap around my ankle, and I waved goodbye to Joey taking comfort in the fact that she would not be able to distinguish me in the river and observe my terrible swimming style.

After waiting in line at the start, I walked onto the plain barge and climbed into the Hudson River with my age group. Other competitors already in the water held a rope stretched across the length of the barge, and I soon found out why. The current almost pulled me over. I grabbed the rope as a handhold prior to the horn blowing. The current continued to yank me into the rope, and I nearly flipped over the other side. Thankfully, I stayed right side up for even Michael Phelps would have a difficult time swimming to the barge against the current in the Hudson.

It hadn't crossed my mind to place my goggles over my eyes before plunging into the water (I always remembered subsequently). I struggled to tug them downwards into position with one hand while holding the rope with the other. I needed to ensure good suction and unimpaired vision. I barely accomplished this feat when the horn blew. And we were off!

I endeavored to swim slowly but got caught up in the excitement and churning of everyone else around me. I went out faster than I ought to, and within 100m, a full panic attack set in. I gasped, trying not to swallow water (*Ew, the Hudson!*) and strained to swim. I reached the 300m mark before I attempted to put my face in the water. I kept fighting the panic attack, sloppily executing the sidestroke and breast stroke, and trying to mix in freestyle. I felt like I was drowning every time my face was underwater because I couldn't seem to get enough air. Breathing in the freestyle stroke is rhythmic. I was "air hungry" and hyperventilating, which shattered any hope of rhythmic breathing. As I swam by the 800m sign marker, I was calm enough to start swimming and began settling into a groove.

Groups of swimmers left the barge every three minutes. Wave after wave of swimmers swam over me. I tried to brace myself when I saw them coming, knowing I was about to be clawed and likely kicked in the face. They swam over top of me. Finally, I saw the 1500m marker. I expected the finish to be near the wall, but it wasn't. A second barge floated located out from shore with a large stairway extending into the water. I paddled over, and someone helped me up. Yee-haw!!

I peeled my wetsuit down to my waist and then ran the 400 yards to the TA entrance. I saw Joey as I came out of the water. I threw my hands in the air and cheered, glad I finished the swim. I knew it would be awful, and it was. On a side note, my swim split for 800m at the sprint triathlon was 23:24 minutes and my swim split for the 1500m at NYC was 23:10. Twice as long and twice as fast; I love an aggressive current!

I ran to my bike and noticed the scorching sun beating down on my head. I stood putting the finishing touches on my bike about to take off my wetsuit when I heard some girls talking about an injury. Being a physician assistant, I walked over to make sure people were okay. One girl discussed how a jellyfish stung a competitor three times in the face.

Jellyfish? I asked if the person was okay, though the girls were unsure.

Apparently, jellyfish had come in close to the coastline during the night or during the race. Multiple people suffered stings. Sadly, one swimmer had a reaction to the jellyfish sting and died. I didn't get stung because my face was out of the water for half of the race. My open water panic for the first 500m probably saved me. I'm fairly certain I would have aborted the race if I had been stung. God works everything for good (Romans 8:28, NIV). *Thank You, God!*

Joey created a sign for me at the Expo the day before, decorated with stickers and streamers. She carried it everywhere on race day starting with the cab ride at 3:30 a.m. I looked for her and her sign while biking and waved twice at her as I rode by the spectator area.

I loved the bike course though traversing the slippery expansion grates on the bridge into the Bronx made the trip harrowing. I tried not to draft but the volume of race participants made this difficult. Drafting, or being within four bike lengths of the person in front of you, is illegal and can earn a penalty as the drafter has less wind resistance. I finished the bike course and changed in the TA.

I jogged into Central Park, my old training ground. My sore legs made running more challenging. I raced 10Ks before, but my legs felt like I had twenty-pound weights around my ankles. I put up a solid performance on the run, and I finished the race in less than three hours. Heading into the finishing shoot at the south end of Central Park with people three deep on either side cheering was an awesome feeling. I had such a sense of accomplishment, a release of tension, and genuine happiness.

I met up with some friends from the city afterwards who showered me with compliments. We snapped some photos and went to grab some food. I love a burger after a race! It replenishes the protein and calories spent and tastes so good after all the sweet Gatorade.

After lunch Joey (still carrying her sign) and I retrieved Lucy. I was leery about throwing Lucy into the back of a cab without her box, so we trekked the five or six miles from the West Side rolling my bike the whole way. We carried a garbage bag filled with my wetsuit, shoes, and remaining gear. I saw the sign she made leaning up against the wall in her apartment the next day when I left. I calculated she carried that sign for nearly twelve hours.

The bike shop guy dismantled my bike, and I flew home. Self-sufficiency can be the name of the game sometimes, and I put Lucy back together again in North Carolina. It took me hours but provided a small victory for me. I finally got to relax for a bit.

The NYC Tri took place in July. Ironman registration for the next year's race starts the day following the current year's race. If I wanted to race Ironman Wisconsin in 2009, I had to register online the day after the race in September 2008. Wisconsin is within driving distance for my parents; I had informed them their presence was mandatory. I had two months to think about things before registering for the 2009 race.

Unbelievably, Ironman registration can sell out within hours. Shockingly, masses of people want to do this, but volunteers get first pick. People will volunteer at the prior year's race in order to get dibs on race spots early the next morning (I told you it was a cult). I didn't have that option. I figured if I didn't get in online, that was God's way of telling me this wasn't the plan.

September came. I had entered registration day on my calendar. I worked that day and was worried I would get a slew of patients at noon and not be able to register. I logged in at 12:00 p.m., but Wisconsin is Central Time. After my false start, I had to wait another hour. I half hoped I wouldn't get a spot, and the race would be full. After the next hour passed, registration opened, and I filled in all the blanks. I hit the submit button. My registration went through immediately. My stomach sank. A slight nausea ensued. Here we go.

What was I thinking?

CHAPTER 15

SPIRITUAL AND PHYSICAL TRAINING

AFTER I MOVED TO NORTH Carolina in December of 2008, I recognized my need to find a church. I saw an ad for Christ Community Church in the newspaper. The first time I attended a service, I sobbed during all four worship songs. The catharsis mimicked what I felt in front of the Jesus statue in New York, only on a larger scale. The kind people, the friendly smiles, and the warm atmosphere all gave the impression of home, and I felt safe. Through a promotional event, I joined a small group and developed more Christian friendships. Suddenly, God filled my life with people who highly valued their relationship with Him.

Loving God wasn't my problem; I didn't love myself. I tried everything in my power to fix this. You name it, and I tried it. Nothing worked. Nothing. When I turned to God, I began to understand the depth of His love for me and how the gospel applied to my life. Only then, was I able to begin to love myself.

Spiritual teaching occurred simultaneously with physical training. During the first few months of 2009, I started tithing. The Bible commands us to give the first tenth of our earnings or a tithe (and to give joyfully). Giving back to God took an incredible leap of faith for me. The first month, I had twenty bucks left over in my budget after donating to church. I didn't purchase anything extraneous, set aside money for gifts, or budget for my Wisconsin trip. I had no money for furniture to fill my empty new house. I said, *Okay God, I'm going to trust You, but You're going to have to take care of everything.* I let go.

Money, necessities, and food fell from the sky. I bought a beautiful bedroom set when I refinanced my house and got an unexpected $2600 in escrow back. I received a free grill when my friend Eileen bought a new house which had its own grill (Alison drove the extra grill forty-five miles to my house without me even asking).

The people at work asked, "Does anyone want this food? Here, Kelly, you take it," at times when the budget approached zero. Once I walked down the stairs at church and thought about how I didn't have groceries to bring for lunch that week, and someone handed me a leftover pizza from a meeting at church.

Yes, in order to tithe, I have to budget but I always seem to have just enough. I continued to increase my giving because it brought me happiness to share. In just one year, God changed my entire way of looking at my finances. God is like that.

My "official" training began December 1, 2008. Darkness enveloped me that first morning when I headed to the gym at 5:00 a.m., and I wondered if I would ever get used to it. Though I figured I wouldn't feel prepared for Ironman Wisconsin, I wanted to give training my best effort. My friend Maggie (from the fast lane at the pool) contacted me and asked if I wanted to race New Orleans 70.3 in April 2009, which is half of the Ironman distance or a half-Ironman (simple, I know). This worked out perfectly with my training plan.

I also registered for the White Lake half-iron distance race four weeks after the New Orleans half-Ironman in May 2009. It wasn't an official Ironman race and, therefore, couldn't be labeled 70.3, but the competition was the same distance (who knew that 70.3, 140.6, and Ironman are copyrighted phrases?). If I was unable to complete New Orleans, then I had White Lake on the schedule.

My training program consisted of twenty weeks for the half-ironman, a two or three-week recovery bridge, and then twenty weeks of Ironman training. I didn't think at all about the race in Wisconsin at this point. The half-Ironman had me shaking in my boots. Wisconsin sat far in the distance while New Orleans loomed right in front of me.

I ran past kids waiting for the school bus on the corners in my neighborhood. I guess kids in North Carolina have to get to school early. Sometimes I nearly ran them over. I couldn't see them well in the dark with their dark hoodies, but thankfully, I avoided collisions in my trusty reflective compression tights and reflective vest.

The first few months of training are always killer. It felt like I sucked at everything, and I would never get it. I remember the drudgery in the pool in the mornings and running at 5 or 6:00 a.m. in the freezing dark. I felt like I was swimming against a current or riding straight into a wind tunnel. Everything was hard. Everything hurt. Everything was fatigued. I mean, even my toenails were tired. But then, after a few months, a workout came along, and I noticed I still had gas left in the tank. This was a milestone where I "rounded the bend." It takes a while to create a solid foundation before really building depth into an athlete's fitness. Moments like these produce confidence.

Unfortunately, a lot of people, and I'm not talking about Ironman racers here, quit during this very important yet difficult foundational period. If one wants to be good at something, they need innate talent. If they're not laden with innate talent, then one must work hard and pay their dues. Payment involves sweat, pain, time, and tears. Preparing for success requires hard work and an attitude of never giving up.

I thought an April race would bring perfect weather in New Orleans. What I didn't realize was an April race would have me training through the coldest part of the year, including open water swimming. Typically, I taper for two to four weeks before the race, so the open water swims would need to be in March or February. Thankfully, Alison borrowed a wetsuit, and we swam in a lake together at our friend, Jill's, house in 47-degree weather. That's cold. I borrowed booties and wore two swim caps. Alison's feet were numb. Jill and her family thought we were crazy. (Jill has since completed an Ironman and is now a coach! It's a cult, I tell you!)

I planned to drive the twelve hours to New Orleans on a Friday. Gear check in was on Saturday, and the race was Sunday. That gave me

Monday to drive home. I hadn't even thought about asking someone to go with me until two friends, Lisa and Suzanne, contacted me and told me they wished to ride along and support me during the race. I couldn't believe it! I was floored.

I owned a Mitsubishi Eclipse which has more than enough room for Lucy in the hatchback and my stuff on the floor, but there isn't room for two other people and their stuff. We talked about renting a car, but I didn't have a bike rack. Alison was kind enough to let me borrow her SUV.

We drove down to New Orleans, and the three of us split the driving. I tried to drive as much as possible because I would probably rest on the way back due to sore legs. Maggie met us in New Orleans, and we all shared a hotel room. We were crammed wall to wall with bikes and bags. My friends willingly slept on a tiny pull out couch. I couldn't ask for better peeps.

Finally, my first big race day was here. Let me digress for a moment again. I race for a lot of reasons. I actually enjoy training. I find satisfaction in setting a goal, creating a plan to achieve that goal, and then systematically working through it until the finish. I like routine. I appreciate regimen. I relish a challenge. Life is boring when we sit around unchallenged and unstimulated, feeling sad and depressed. When people sit in their comfort zones with nowhere to focus their energies, they turn inward. It happens to me, too. But I prefer to extend myself outwards, on a path heading toward a specific goal.

I like being outdoors and working my muscles. I enjoy exercise, the stress relief it gives, and the "high" I get afterwards. A well-executed workout creates a sense of satisfaction. I recharge spending time alone. True, seven hours alone on the bike training for an Ironman is a little much, but it was never too much for me to handle. In fact, it's where God gave me the words to write. My brain can run continually in the background while being focused on the task at hand.

Race Week is another reason I love to race. Excitement and nervous energy course through my vessels. The race I strived for is finally here.

I get to lay it all on the line. Fear also rears its ugly head, and I become scared I will underperform, not be able to finish, or will somehow disappoint myself. After working so hard for so long, I know these things would devastate me.

This internal tug-of-war creates "the storm." Have you ever seen a weather forecast on TV where they show a cartoonish picture of the hurricane spinning off the coast? It looks like a donut of white going around and around as it gets closer to land. I feel the same storm inside my gut. The hurricane is inside my inner being, maybe even in my soul. It starts to spin, this storm of excitement and fear. I feel every cell of my body. I am aware of everything I experience on a visceral level. It's hyper-awareness akin to the hairs on the back of your neck standing straight up. It's being alive to the fullest extent. The numbness and the monotony of life all fall away. And what is left is an extreme focus, an unwavering line of sight which exists between me and my goal: the race.

Racing reduces me to a primordial level. It somehow delineates the boundaries that outline my space in the world and claim it for me. I train because I love it (granted, I don't love *every* 4:30 a.m. workout). When I race, I am my true self to the fullest degree, and I encounter this in racing more than in anything else I have ever done. I'm 100% me and pushing it all the way as hard as I can. Others may race for different reasons. I race because I love the storm that builds, and I love to set it free.

CHAPTER 16

THE FIRST HALVES

ON SATURDAY, MAGGIE AND I dropped off our gear, which took hours. Suzanne and Lisa went off to enjoy New Orleans. My mom called that afternoon when my emotions were running high, and I could only respond to her questions with "yes" or "no" to avoid breaking into sobs. There's no crying in Ironman. I prayed and prayed.

God please get me through this. I don't feel strong enough.

Finally, the sun rose on race day. Maggie and I woke up and performed our pre-race routine, which included eating peanut butter and honey on whole wheat English muffins in the hallway so as not to wake Suzanne and Lisa. Suzanne heard us anyway and came into the hallway to wish us luck. We headed over to the transition area and to the race start. We walked along the entire 1.2 miles of the swim course, which was a point-to-point swim (starts and finishes in different locations as opposed to a loop or an out-and-back). Thankfully, the buoys were out!

As we rambled along, walking and walking, I thought to myself, *man, this is far.* I forced myself to refocus and told myself, *you only have to swim to the next buoy, no farther than the next buoy.*

Keep in mind the half-ironman was only my third triathlon. We arrived at the start line and went into the swim corral. Maggie was one age group behind me. While we waited, a fellow competitor said, "Just enjoy the water."

Yes, I thought, *that's what I will do.* We lined up in the water, and I told myself repeatedly, *go slowly and avoid the panic.* Then, the horn sounded.

A sort of inner peace ensues once a race starts. The worry fades since no more preparation is possible. The clock is running; all I can do is go.

Unfortunately, I didn't go out as slowly as I should have—again. By the first buoy, I was out of breath.

Other swimmers took off swimming fast; I took off breathing fast. My journey through the first three out of ten buoys involved a lot of sidestroke, swimming on my side with my face out of the water. I had promised myself that no matter what, I would keep moving.

As I struggled and gasped, my competitor's words floated back to me, "Just enjoy the water."

Yes, *enjoy the water,* I told myself. Four strokes later the voice in my head screamed, *No! I hate this! I hate the water!* with a few expletives thrown in. I thought of transitioning to long distance duathlons, run-bike-run with no swim, because I felt defeated.

In the mandatory pre-race meeting Maggie and I attended the day before, the speaker let us know we could opt out of the swim. If athletes felt the water was too choppy or believed they could not complete the swim safely, competitors would be corralled for a short period of time and then released into transition.

Swimming is not easy, and I do struggle with balance in the water and stroke technique. I resolved not to give in and quit simply because swimming was difficult for me. Incidentally, Maggie turned to me at this point in the pre-race meeting and said sternly, "Don't even think about it."

Now, that's the love of a good friend.

One day, I hope to be a shark in the water. Until that day, I will continue being the turtle I've always been. Throughout the race I developed a sort of pattern of swim, swim, swim, stop, float, sight, swim, swim, swim, stop, float, sight, etc. A multitude of swimmers passed me, probably from about four groups behind me. I swallowed the humble pie and kept going. The reality was no one cared how I swam except me. Soon, I saw the wonderful orange buoy signaling the turn into the beach. Two things ran through my mind:

1. *Thank You, Jesus!*

2. *Lucy, I'm coming!*

My average heart rate was 165 for the swim, 149 for the bike, and 143 for the run. My swim panic accelerated my pulse by close to 20 points, which shows how much anxiety can affect us physiologically.

I finished the 1800m swim in a whopping fifty-three minutes; Maggie came in at thirty-seven minutes, and my time was probably the slowest of the race. But I finished. When I wasn't sure I could do it, I finished. When I struggled and when thoughts of quitting played in the back of my mind, I didn't. When I wanted to cry, I gutted it out to the end. I'm so proud of that swim time!

I jogged from the water to my bike, and she hung by herself on the rack. Thankfully, Lucy doesn't have much of an ego and isn't bothered by being the last bike hanging.

The race planners streamlined the finishers into one cluster by scheduling the male start times behind the women in the race. Men traditionally race faster than women, so the setup had all finishers clumped together.

Many of the male racers rode bikes with solid back wheels (or disc wheels) created to decrease resistance and increase speed. The wheels produce a "whoomp, whoomp, whoomp" sound I got used to as the boys cycled by. My game plan on the bike was to go easy and enjoy the scenery. I love to look for animals when riding and frequently shout, "Hi, guys," while waving at cows (cows are my favorite!).

Guess what I saw in New Orleans? One stinking butterfly and maybe one bird. That was it. Not even a squirrel. The bike course was the most boring fifty-six miles I have ever ridden. The aid stations were out of water and Gatorade as I finished the segment, so I had to make my water last. In addition, 20-30 mph headwinds pummeled the riders. I averaged 16.8 mph, which wasn't bad considering my training ride average was 15 mph in December.

I ate too many Cliff bars and Shot Blocks early in the bike leg, and they sat in my stomach like a brick. My insides cramped any time I tried to bend forward in my aerobars; an aerodynamic position would have helped in the headwinds.

The weather prediction on race day had been for thunderstorms at 2:00 to 3:00 p.m. I did not want to struggle through the long swim only to get hauled off the bike course due to lightning. Hence, I put my mom on it. My mom has this weird fascination with weather. I don't know if it's part of getting older, but she talks about it all of the time.

Whatever the reason, she has God on speed dial when it comes to weather. He hears my mom's meteorologic prayers. I'm serious. Instead of rain, the sun blazed down at eighty degrees out of a cloudless sky. The first few miles of the run were like running in a desert, reminiscent of the Chicago marathon. The next time I asked my mom to pray for weather, I requested she be a little more moderate.

As I began those first few miles of the run, I realized I had 3.5 hours before the cutoff, so I walked/ran to help with the heat. The triathlete in me was happy, though the runner in me cringed. I picked up the pace during the second half as trees provided more shade. Suzanne and Lisa planted themselves on the course in at least eight different spots to cheer me on.

Somewhere near the end, people cheered, "You're almost there! You're almost there!"

Reader, let me school you on something for a moment. When racing 70.3 miles or even 26.2 miles, "there" means the point when the racer gets to fall down and rest. "There" is the destination the athlete struggles for against their own sanity. Two more miles is not "almost there." "Almost there" means the finish line is in view, and rest is imminent. When people kept saying, "You're almost there," I craned my neck to look around. *Where is it?*

Finally, I saw the finish line! Mike Reilly, the voice of Ironman, called my name as I completed 70.3 miles of racing. Maggie found me in the crowd, and we shared a sweaty, smiling hug. We looked at the posted splits. My final time was 6:41:11. My goal had been under eight hours. I ran my finger down the paper over my swim time of fifty-three minutes. Like in football, sometimes it's not about winning; it's about finishing.

I'm proud of those fifty-three minutes. Two years prior to this race, I couldn't swim at all. Now, I swam 1.2 miles in a half-Ironman race, which puts me in a small percentage of people. My finish time is mine forever, and no one can take it from me. Despite fear, doubts, and panic, I was an Ironman 70.3.

What did I learn from this race? Buoys, disc wheels, and per mile averages? No, I learned I have great friends. It started with Lisa and Suzanne and included Alison letting me drive her car all the way to New Orleans and offering her bicycle tires the day before I left (I realized my tires were cracking; who knew I had to check my tires?). As cheerleaders, Suzanne and Lisa stalked me on the race course. When we drove out of New Orleans, they asked if they could be my groupies, and I almost cried.

When the race was over, I felt considerable relief. I did it! I could do it! I relaxed and then began to plan for the next half Ironman, which took place four weeks later. I prepared a two to three-week training bridge before the White Lake Half Ironman, which involved both rest and training. Athletes throw down their longest and hardest workouts a few weeks before a race. This peak is followed by a taper lasting several weeks where one eases up tremendously allowing his or her muscles to heal.

Having another race so quickly presented challenges. I felt I couldn't rest at this point in order to keep my fitness at a high level (though I probably could have). Mentally, I was in better shape than during the previous half ironman. In every triathlon up until this point, I attempted more advanced races each time. White Lake was the first time I repeated a distance, which gave me some comfort. The training bridge worked well, and I felt confident going into the race.

I drove to the race with Alison, who raced on Sunday in a sprint triathlon at the same location. The half-Ironman occurred the Saturday before her race. I appreciated that I would get my race out of the way first and be able to enjoy and focus on supporting Alison. We awoke at oh-dark-thirty in the inky black darkness. The generators hummed, and the triathletes scurried around their bikes in the transition area like swarming insects. Alison's neighbor, Melissa, had a friend who planned to race named Rachel.

Alison introduced me to Rachel, who told me this was her third triathlon ever (*Ah, a kindred spirit*). She completed a super sprint and a sprint previously and now entered a half Ironman. Tears streamed down Rachel's face at the thought of racing over seventy miles (*See? It's not just me*). Having just finished New Orleans, I knew exactly how she felt. I reassured her that she would be fine, and the race wasn't as far as it seemed. We became instantaneous friends, bonded by our ridiculous ambitions which were underscored by a lack of talent. We forever joke about being "mediocre" people.

Everyone, and I mean everyone, needs a Rachel in their life. Whatever your passion is, you can benefit from a Rachel. I decided to compete in an Ironman before I could swim. Rachel jumped from the sprint distance to the half Ironman distance; she is full of unabashed courage. Many men do not have the fearless attitude she has. Every totally ridiculous race, ride, or run I have ever wanted to do, I could count on Rachel to do it with me. Rachel is all heart.

As our friendship grew, we trained for several race events. Then she became pregnant with her fourth child. Oh, did I forget to mention that? Rachel was a triathlete and a mother of three children (under six years of age) with a husband who traveled during the week. Whatever excuse people have for not exercising, please let me know, and I will provide Rachel's email address for some tips.

Now we both faced the White Lake Half in the middle of North Carolina. We entered the water and waited with our age group. When the start horn blared, my palms were dry and my heart rate normal. I totally enjoyed the swim without any panic. I sliced through the water at my pace and watched the sun rise with each breath.

Dr. Thomas Fuller says in *Gnomologia* in 1732, "All things are difficult before they are easy."[12] In our world of immediate gratification, we often forget that sacrifice precludes mastery: I had to pay my dues.

During the swim, I reached a plateau whereas prior to this, I fought an uphill battle. Open water swimming became my favorite swim workout through the rest of my training, and I typically swam at Jill's house once a week. Jill, Alison, and I would climb down Jill's dock ladder into the dark water and watch the sun come up over the trees in the quiet of the morning. Because God carried me through my struggle with open water swimming, I planned my adult baptism in the open water.

After the White Lake swim, I ran down the dock and up the grassy hill to the transition area and put on my cycling gear. The bike course was flat allowing higher speeds, but the runners baked in the sun running on the backside of people's fences. We ran the same three mile out-and-back twice, and there was very little scenery. I took twenty-six minutes off my total time from New Orleans. The confidence I had in myself to finish made me faster. Life is difficult when we face the unknown, lack trust in God, and bet our chips on ourselves. God brought me through the other races, and He would lead me through this one. At the time, I did not have spiritual clarity and was blind to God's part in my racing. I saw only me.

Alison and I waited for Rachel to finish. Her nemesis is the bike, and she undertrained for this race. This mother of three smiled as she crossed the finish line. Rachel and I cheered Alison on the next day, and she finished strong. The blue skies contained fluffy clouds, and a peaceful light breeze blew the entire weekend. White Lake was the last weekend before I faced the beast, before my official Ironman Wisconsin training began. The last twenty weeks.

CHAPTER 17

THE DAYS BEFORE

UNFORTUNATELY, I MET RACHEL TOO late for her to register for Wisconsin. I arranged my training realizing most of the workouts would be solo; I didn't know anyone who wanted to cycle or run such long distances while exercising. I housed my training plan in a black, three-ring binder. I carried it with me everywhere like a security blanket. I fit workouts in around social activities and crammed church events in between. I juggled life as best I could. Once I rode my bike after work, took a bird bath rinse in a Shell gas station bathroom, and then attended a wedding shower dinner. Life was crazy. My binder became so battered by the end, scotch tape held it together.

I usually arose at 5:00 a.m. to exercise and worked out again after leaving my job. Most days had two workouts, a few days had one, and usually I had one day off per week (but not always). Three to five 100-mile bike rides waited for me at the end of the training schedule. The last day in this planner was race day.

When I signed up for Wisconsin, I chose the race without doing much research. Madison was close enough that my family could drive there, and the Midwest is flat. Well, not entirely. Unfortunately, they hold the race in Dane County, which is exceptionally hilly. I told someone at church, who also raced, that I chose Ironman (IM) Wisconsin.

"You picked a hard one," he said.

"Come again?" It turns out, there is approximately 6,000 feet of climbing (riding a bike uphill) I wasn't aware of when I registered. I inadvertently picked a difficult Ironman race out of ignorance. However,

I had locked in my registration, and there was only one thing I could do: Suck it up and ride hills.

I drove over an hour with my bike to ride 100 miles of hills in various parts of North Carolina; the rides lasted 7-8 hours. A short run followed; after which I hopped back in the car for the long drive home. This was all so I could ride on bigger hills. I frequented a 15-mile route in a nearby town with some hills, and I forced myself to stay in the big ring, or the larger front gear, on the bike in order to build leg strength. Pushing a bigger gear is more difficult. I scoured local and regional areas for hills; I would find them and ride them. My whole Saturday consisted of driving and riding and then driving home only to flop nearly comatose on the couch.

The weather was hot as all get out because I lived in the South. I carried six bottles of water for a 50-mile ride once only to get back to the car and reload my bottles to ride another 50 miles. I felt like a pack mule. I rode in thunderstorms with lightning and complete downpours. Why stop? The rain already soaked me, and the car was parked 40 miles away. Sometimes the dark skies poured, and water drained to the heel of my shoe as I pedaled up an incline and then sloshed down to my toes once I crested the climb. I had a farmer's tan that couldn't be rivaled.

Sweat crystallized in dense clumps on the sides of my face. The crystals felt like daggers scraping against my skin. I had saddle sores (boils) on my backside from sitting in the bike seat so long. I lost toenails (who needs 'em) and had blisters. I wore duct tape on my feet when I ran. My friends and I swam at Jill's house on the lake before the sun came up wearing glow sticks stuck in our goggle straps, so we could find each other in the pitch-black darkness. Training whipped my body into shape. Fear of failure drove me to sacrifice my "today" for what I could become "tomorrow."

God spoke to me on my long rides. He provided all the words for this book, all the text for another fictional novel, and inspiration for so many other things.

"Those who dream by day are cognizant of many things which escape those who dream only by night," says Edgar Allan Poe in 'Eleanora' in 1842.[13] God shared my brain space with me while I cycled. Being on the road for so long enabled me to develop a "standby" mental mode. As I pedaled the bicycle, part of my brain shut off as muscle memory assumed control of the reins. This left quiet and peace for God to speak to me and inspire my writing.

I discerned on a deep, internal level that completing the Ironman would require God's power. Depending on God was my only hope. Easy in theory, difficult in practice. In my mind, I felt I trusted God, but, in reality, I still worked in my own strength. My faith was inadequate. I called my mom one day, sobbing a big, ugly cry about how I wouldn't be able to finish the Ironman.

"Well, you don't have to go if you don't want to."

I almost shouted, "That's not what you're supposed to say!" I called so she could urge me to shut up, get up, and get going! Instead, I went back to the binder and kept digging into my training sessions. My fear of failure grew, becoming unbearable. I worried about failure almost constantly. In the book *In Pharaoh's Army*, Tobias Wolff writes, "We are made to persist. That's how we find out who we are."[14]

I barely hung on.

In my small group at church, my friend, Shannon, mentioned she needed help with the youth small groups. I have zero patience and said to myself, *Oh, I could never do that.* I felt God smiling and whispering, "When is she going to get this?"

I couldn't escape God's prompting, so I volunteered to help. I aspired to serve at church and here was a need. I emailed several friends regarding how freaked out I was about leading a youth small group and how completely unqualified I was to teach anybody anything.

One replied, "Sometimes God qualifies the called."

God communicated my way to me. He calls; I follow. He commands; I obey. This is the path; this is how it works. I struggle with this lesson today, repeatedly trying to pave my own trail.

My training built and built on each level like stair steps until I finally hit my taper. When my workout volume decreased, and my rest increased during the taper period, all the energy I previously expended was now conserved. The energy bounced inward, and a roar started to build inside me. Not like the MGM lion roar. More like the Incredible Hulk roar.

I'm probably dating myself here, but Bill Bixby (*The Incredible Hulk*) used to say, "You won't like me when I'm angry." Then his eyes turned white and high-pitched music blared in the background of the scene. All of a sudden, his body would metamorphose with enlarging green muscles tearing through all his clothes (except his pants, which always really puzzled me as a child because Bill Bixby had skinny thighs and Lou Farigno had giant thighs). After the transformation, the giant, green-skinned Hulk raised his arms in the air, brought them down in a bodybuilding pose, and roared.

This is the roar I'm talking about. I feel this roar in a taper or at the end of a killer workout. An "Incredible Hulk roar" wells up inside me. And to be honest, at the end of some of my kick butt long training sessions, I did roar.

These momentary roars didn't quell the overriding fear, however. I endured a three-week period near the end of training where I cried every day, multiple times a day. Training is a series of builds; I never completed the full Ironman distance because it would take too much time to recover. Instead, I built workout upon workout and hoped in the end that I did enough. I needed to trust God would be with me on race day, but I'm a performance junkie. I'm a doer who is arrogant and relies on myself. Relinquishing control was difficult.

Then, the end of training arrived. I moved my "You can do it!" sticky tab to the last week of my binder. For weeks it seemed I would be mired in training forever. Anticipation encircled me.

I packed up Lucy and flew to Chicago. My parents picked me up at O'Hare Airport and drove me and my stuff to Madison. I couldn't get a direct flight to Madison and was nervous about losing Lucy during a plane transfer. My mind swirled with things that could be "total game changers." I was so close to achieving my goal, I incessantly thought of roadblocks which could potentially waylay me, i.e. flat tires, Lucy getting lost, coming down with the flu, etc. I didn't want the hours and weeks and months of sacrifice to be for nothing. If I crashed and burned, I wanted to fail bleeding, crying, and crawling my knees toward the finish line and not because an airline sabotaged my race by losing my baby girl, Lucy.

When I boxed her up, I, unfortunately, had a screaming fit at Alison. This was not my finest hour. I felt let down by her, and I let her have it. I share this with my readers, so they know I am human like everyone and not some super person who can do things others can't. God used my Ironman training to teach me. I struggled, yelled, and was self-focused. God uses the ugly in us, too.

On Lucy's box I plastered a note which read, "This is my bike. Her name is Lucy. Please take good care of her." My parents reached Madison without a hitch, and my mom waited with me in the baggage area for my belongings. I carried all my race gear, expertly packed, with me on the plane, so I would be able to race in the event they lost my luggage. My checked bags appeared on the conveyor, and, eventually, the luggage carriage stopped. No big bike box, no Lucy. I went to a set of double doors and peered inside. A guy walked out, and I explained I was looking for my bike. He disappeared. Minutes went by. Another guy appeared, and I explained the story again in an increasingly panicked tone.

He smiled and said, "Are you looking for Lucy?" (*Thank You, Jesus*).

"Yes, I'm looking for Lucy," I smiled. He brought her out, and we loaded her in the SUV and darted off to Madison.

I reassembled my bike in the hotel room, but I couldn't get the handlebars on straight. I panicked (again). I also couldn't work my dad's bike pump, which he brought since my pump didn't fit into my suitcase. The inability to pump up my tires was the straw that broke the camel's back. I had a meltdown verbally vomiting my frustration all over my parents. Oh, how the people around me suffered! People act dreadful sometimes when they're stressed, and I'm not immune.

Finally, my mom grabbed some guy in the hallway, and he pumped up my bike tires. Thankfully, my parents forgave me. They understood because they were as nervous as I was for the race.

I had the opportunity to swim part of the swim course before race day and get a feel for the water, which was murky with green algae floating on the surface. I finished my short session of paddling, and my mom stood holding a towel *("Aww, thanks, Mom!")*. My parents and I drove the bike course to prepare for the bike segment. We circled the loop once, and the 56 miles took one and a half hours in a car. I had to complete the loop twice during the race. I sat in the backseat clasping my hands in a death grip as I worried about what was to come.

Expectation and excitement ushered in the eve of race day. I breathed a sigh of relief when Alison arrived at the hotel for support. The adrenaline made me super sensitive to everything. Anticipation bounced off the walls and bombarded me like electricity in the air. I went into the bathroom and felt the energy ricocheting around the small room. Thankfully, one of my favorite pastimes distracted me: watching college football. Lucky for me, my Michigan Wolverines beat Notre Lame (misspelling intentional).

I dropped off my bike and transition gear. Each athlete had a bag labeled "Bike" and "Run." After the swim, competitors would run to the "Transition Area" where they would change in separate male and female areas and have access to their "Bike" bags. After changing, the athletes clip-clopped in cycling shoes out to the bike racks. When the athletes completed the cycling, they went back to the transition area to grab their "Run" bags.

I practiced each transition, running the hallways and routes in the facility I would take on race day. I stared at my setup and mentally ran through my equipment changes again and again. Then I left as there was nothing more to do. After standing in a huge line at Applebee's, we ordered dinner to go. I went to sleep reasonably early that night, after filling up on pasta marinara and setting multiple alarms. I wonder how I ever fell asleep.

PART THREE

OFF TO THE RACES

CHAPTER 18

THE BEAST

I HAD MY MINUTE-TO-MINUTE RACE day plan typed and ready to go, which detailed everything I would do from the moment I woke up. You can find this write-up in the next chapter and will hopefully appreciate how incredibly OCD I am. That morning, Alison and I arose at 4:00 a.m. and started making coffee. My parents awoke at 3:30 a.m. Anxiety tends to alter my parents' morning routine. The coffeemaker in my room did not work, which caused a flare of stress, but my dad went downstairs and retrieved coffee for me from the lobby, thereby rescuing the morning.

We headed over to the location for the "Special Needs" bag drop. Approximately halfway through the bike route and halfway through the run, Ironman races have a place where racers can pick up a "Special Needs" bag and have a snack or change clothes. Luckily, we found the appropriate area, and I jumped from the car to drop off my stuff. The sky was pitch black, and the adrenaline pumping through my arteries had the hair on my arms standing on end. I can still feel the chill in the air as I bent over the box to place my gear bag inside. We parked in a garage right near the TA and walked over.

I proceeded to Lucy to get her ready to roll. I had trouble with my dad's tire pump again. (Sidebar: why can I operate my own bike pump without *any* issue but not my dad's?) I borrowed another pump and inflated my tires. I filled my aero bottle with Gatorade, put my other water bottles in the racks, and taped my nutrition gel packs to my top tube. I stared at my bike for a while, working through things in my mind as part of my ritual. Bikes seemed to extend to the horizon.

119

Mike Reilly's voice resonated over the PA with various announcements. Mike Reilly is the voice of Ironman. He would potentially call me an Ironman in less than seventeen hours.

I left Lucy and headed to body marking, which I love. Having a volunteer write your number on your shoulders and thighs is like putting on war paint. I asked my volunteer to pen, "Phil. 4:13" on my right calf. The verse references, "I can do all this through him who gives me strength" in the NIV version. I acknowledged my faith publicly while racing and having a Bible verse on my leg helped to calm me.

After getting my body marked, Alison, my mom, my dad, and I made a last bathroom pit stop before I dropped off my last bag with the clothes I wore to the start over my racing outfit (there were a lot of bags). I put on my body glide to prevent chafing at the joints and edges of my wetsuit. My parents asked, "Why are you putting deodorant on your wrists?"

Body glide comes in a deodorant-like container. I chuckled to myself. As part of the racing cult, athletes understand "inside" things others do not. I forget sometimes I'm part of the "cult." I inched into my wetsuit.

I wore my bike shorts and triathlon tank top with my wetsuit over top. I tucked an extra set of goggles inside the front of my wetsuit and placed my cap and other goggles on my head. I gave Alison and my parents a half-wave and walked through the athlete gate. I had watched a video of a previous IM Wisconsin and in the beginning, one girl cried all the way to the swim start. When I watched it, I thought, *Man, I hope I'm not that scared. I don't want to cry like she did.* I would have cried if I said a big goodbye to my parents, so I avoided eye contact. Not only because fear gripped me, but because the whole experience was so much to take in.

I crossed the swim check-in mat at around 6:40 a.m., which logged my presence at the start line. I barely noticed any of my surroundings because I felt so scared. I focused on breathing. People treaded water in the lake, but I didn't want to expend energy before the race as I find treading water extremely tiring. I walked into the water and stationed myself in a side wading area where I could stand. A nice woman my parents had spoken with while I swam in the practice swim on Friday morning recommended this. With about two minutes to go, I paddled out a bit. Then the cannon went off!

It's quite an experience to have 2,400 athletes all start swimming the same course at exactly the same time. They call it the "washing machine." The swim start paled in comparison to my "mass start" swim practice. About a month prior to the race, I bought snacks and beer and invited friends to harass me while swimming at Jill's house, which was our usual open water swimming location on Lake Norman. A mass start, like the one on race day, is mass chaos. I'm a weak swimmer. I felt if I went through a race start simulation, I would be better prepared. I was right. If you want to get ready for a mass start, I have one word for you . . . Melissa. She is Alison's neighbor, and she took her mass start participant role very seriously. She was all over me in the practice. She grabbed my elbows, swam right next to me, and splashed me. Others pulled at my feet and paddled over top of me. There's a great picture of me with about two dozen friends who tried to sink me during this practice.

After the cannon I swam at an angle toward the course (which was more central in the water) from the shore where I had initially been standing. On the land right next to the lake was a big helical parking structure, called the helix, which led to the transition areas. The helix curved around and around, and spectators lined it from top to bottom cheering and yelling. As I continued to swim, I could look at the fans every time I breathed on my right side. I tried to settle in and recreate the feeling of White Lake and my newfound love of open water swimming. I could never find a groove. I struggled.

I remembered my mantra to swim to the next buoy, but the buoys kept multiplying! As I was looking for the red turn buoy, I thought, *Isn't it almost here yet? Nope, another yellow buoy.* After what seemed like hours, I reached the far end of the course and pretty soon I swam down the back stretch of the rectangle shaped swim course.

At this point I had to urinate. I figured I would try to go in the water once during my second lap as we had to swim the loop twice. My first lap took around fifty-two minutes though looking at my watch proved difficult. All along the next stretch I tried to pee in my wetsuit to save time (ask any endurance triathlete about this common practice and exercise caution when renting a wetsuit). I held my breath and bore down, but nothing worked. I became so focused on urinating I would slow to a stop from concentrating so hard! But it was to no avail. I tried again down the back stretch of the loop, but eventually, I gave up as I was wasting time.

As I rounded the last buoy, I could have screamed! I was almost done with the Ironman swim! I raised my head to view the swim finish and some guy promptly swam over me, plunging me unsuspectingly underwater. He was nice and stopped to ask if I was okay. As I breached the side of the lake at the finish, I looked at my watch. The second loop took me about an hour. I seemed to lose about ten minutes. I stood up on the shore, and though my legs wobbled, my heart felt like it could burst out of my chest. I finished the 2.4-mile swim. Some people can't run that far let alone swim it. I tear up thinking out it. Yahoo!

A volunteer asked me if I was okay as I teetered across the swim finish mat on jelly legs while the gravel shifted precariously under my feet. My vision was cloudy, and I could not see well. I peeled my goggles off my face, but the haziness persisted. I rubbed my eyes trying to see more clearly, and photographers memorialized this pose in every swim finish picture taken of me.

I reached the wetsuit strippers. I hadn't pulled the arms of my wetsuit down as my hands had dealt with my eyes. One volunteer peeled down the arms, and I let go of my cap and goggles, so they would be safely tucked in the sleeve. I laid down and a second volunteer whooshed my wetsuit off. Luckily for them, I had struggled to pee in my wetsuit (a blessing in disguise).

I ran with my wetsuit in hand and figured, *Oh, well, hopefully my vision will clear up.* My eyesight did sharpen by the time I mounted my bike. As I headed through what was previously the athlete gate, I saw Alison and my parents. I yelled, "I didn't drown!" and smiled broadly. I took longer than predicted, and I didn't want them to worry. (I bought a lamp shaped like a turtle to commemorate my Ironman swim!)

After I passed my crew, I ran up the three flights on the helix, around and around and around. Finally, volunteers directed me into the bike bag transition room. I retraced the steps I had practiced, grabbed my bag, and headed into the women's changing area. I picked up a volunteer as I walked in who guided me to a chair and dumped out my bag. Volunteers help everyone change. I selected what I needed; I had over packed my gear bags with things I MAY need JUST IN CASE. I wore my bike shorts and top under my wetsuit, so I needed only my sunglasses, gloves, socks, shoes, and helmet. I click-clacked my way out to the bikes in my bike shoes. I stopped at the port-a-potties on my way to the bike racks.

Lucy hung alone or with one other bike on the rack. Another volunteer brought her to the aisle after being alerted of my race number and thus my bike position. The TA held well over 2,700 projected competitors. Click, clack, click, clack I went, forced to run in my shoes. At the mount line, I hopped on my bike, acutely aware of three things: 1) I was really thirsty, 2) I was hungry, and 3) my legs hurt more than expected after a swim. I realized, as I began pedaling, I had never started a long bike with such a nutritional deficit.

I should have practiced this.

CHAPTER 19

DARK BIKE

I DRANK TWO-THIRDS OF ONE water bottle in the first few minutes on the bike to help stave off dehydration and nutritional depletion. I cursed myself for breaking my own cardinal rule: never do anything on race day you haven't done in practice. I pushed calories for the first few hours praying it would help.

The bike course looked familiar from the dry run in my parent's car. Knowing I headed the right way comforted me. I crested hills to be met by beautiful patch-worked, farmland landscapes and vistas. I verbally encouraged other competitors and concentrated on cycling safely alongside other participants. I pulled hills better than many of the people around me. I'm a better cyclist than I am a swimmer.

I focused on the drafting rule, making sure to stay four bike lengths behind the rider in front of me. To pass, the cyclist following has twenty seconds to overtake the front rider or they need to drop back. I pedaled harder than my plan in order to sprint by people within the designated twenty seconds. I checked in with myself to make sure I wasn't driving the bike at too hard of an average pace for me. After the first two miles, my legs hurt, and I thought, *only 110 more miles to go. Man, this is really far.*

People told me the Ironman race would be an amazing, spiritual experience. A guy in line at packet pick-up said the race "would change my life." All I thought in those first ten miles on the bike was, *how come no one told me how much this was going to suck? I mean, seriously!*

Several years later, I do recall the experience as one of the greatest of my life. Sometimes we must get through events to finally appreciate them.

I decided to give support to others during the race as payback for all the support people had given me. The race bibs had each athlete's name on it. As I passed people I said, "Great job, Michael," or "You're doing great, Trish." I motivated as many as I could and ended up speaking to about ninety percent of the competitors I saw. Most people acted surprised to hear their name. Only one man soured my "great job" comment ye responding, "Not really." Hey buddy, we all suck it up sometimes.

I settled in and worked the hills as they came, which were rough up to this point. Up and down and up and down among the fields and pastures. I arrived at the one-and-a-half-mile downhill on Garfoot and tucked down in my aerobars for the ride. I braked more than usual, nervous that I would wipe out on the steep decline. I didn't struggle this hard in training to lose it all on a dumb move. Bales of hay buffeted some of the more vicious turns to soften wipeouts.

I enjoyed the beautiful farmland and the cows I saw (I smelled more than I saw), but I had to stay focused on the road and other riders, unlike during my training rides. The lead male lapped me at mile twenty-six on the bike, and he littered, throwing an empty gel packet, right in front of me. The lead woman, who ended up winning for the ladies, lapped me at mile fifty-two.

Some of the bigger hills appeared after the turn onto Stagecoach Road. The last ten miles of the loop make the first thirty-five miles seem flat. I practiced on a hill in North Carolina near Crowder's Mountain. Without a downhill to gain momentum, the incline arcs up, and halfway to the top, the grade steeply increases. Someone spray painted the word "Ouch" on the road. I rode up this hill at 6.8 mph with my heart rate jacked into the 180s, huffing and puffing until I crested the hill. I nicknamed this hill "Satan." I hoped Satan would be tougher than any slope I faced in the Ironman race.

I was wrong. Two climbs outmatched Satan by the droves, and two more equaled Satan. These four hideous hills pounded me within the same ten miles at the end of the loop. The massacre my legs endured devastated my mental game after climbing hills, hills, and more hills for forty-five-plus miles only to hit four super-duper climbs, all the while knowing I had to ascend them again the second time around.

Hundreds of people lined these big hills to cheer. I saw their faces, too, because I grinded up those hills at a painful 4.9 mph, standing up out of the saddle. Bystanders walked at a faster pace than I rode, making me wish I had a granny gear on my bike. I congratulated myself for completing a bunch of hill workouts in my big ring (a higher gear) to build strength and confidence. I wouldn't have survived without them.

I headed into the neighborhood of Verona, which was halfway through the bike course. World Triathlon Corporation shuttled spectators to a fenced in area, and I knew I would see my parents and Alison. The race coordinators set up an aid station well, so I had to contend with a bottle exchange instead of soaking in the crowd. I waved at my parents and Alison.

I cycled toward the finish of the second loop and felt demoralized seeing the left turn heading back to the Transition Area while I turned right for the second loop and a repeat of those horrible hills. A dark cloud formed over my psyche, and I couldn't shake the gloom for the whole second loop. I never experienced anything like this, not even during my first marathon in Chicago when the sun radiated a 90-degree heat, and the directors canceled the race. Other athletes told me I would want to quit the Ironman at some point, but I didn't think the feeling would last for forty miles.

After fifty-six miles, my emotions were spent. Failure of my nutritional plan likely contributed to my negative mindset. I expended spiritual energy when encouraging others, and maybe I needed to be filled up again. I also didn't relish the thought of riding those hills again. Any number of factors played into my emotional state; I can't nail down one particular cause. All I do know is I cried on my bike for forty miles. My ego kept me from crying around other competitors, but the tears flowed when I was alone. I bawled about once or twice every ten miles of the second loop.

I said the Lord's Prayer (or the "Our Father" as my Catholic family called it) every time I became upset. I did not stop riding, and I continued to pass people and encourage them. My legs functioned separately from my insides. After I finished the tough hills for the second and last time, relief never came, which pointed to a nutritional or spiritual cause. The bottom line is a very dark cloud hovered over me, and I sobbed lots of lonely tears on the second loop of the Ironman Wisconsin bike course.

Maybe Satan tried to break me, but he didn't win despite my weakness. I finished because God didn't plan for me to fail. Jeremiah 29:11 tells us, "For I know the plans that I have for you,' declares the Lord, 'plans to prosper you and not to harm you, plans to give you hope and a future (NIV).'" I completed the bike portion because God carried me through.

As I approached the difficult and challenging section of the second loop, I worked each of the four hills one by one. Many people walked their bikes up the hill, but I had some gas in my legs yet. If I could ride, then I rode. The crowd support had dwindled as people left to cheer their athletes along the run course. I figured if my legs really hurt and I absolutely couldn't climb the hill, I would stop and walk. But, I was not willing to trudge up the hill just to rest. There would be plenty of time for rest later.

I told my family they could stay and watch me at Verona during the second loop or take the shuttle back to watch the winner finish. At my pace, they waited over three hours to see me ride by twice. As I reached the spectator area, I looked for the tall sign my parents carried. When I saw them, I started to cry again; I sobbed as I rode by. If my mother had been alone on the sideline, I would have stopped and bailed on the race. Thankfully, she stood behind a barricade, out of reach.

Alison sent a text to my friends asking for prayer. Without anywhere else to go, I made the left turn and rode in the last fourteen miles to the TA defeated, nauseated, and with severe abdominal cramping. I forced myself to eat another gel for nutrition, and I nearly vomited to the side of my bike.

Throughout the entire bike course, I leap-frogged back and forth with a girl named Kristi. We would talk briefly whenever one of us passed the other. We cracked a few comments regarding how we felt about those hills as we headed back into Madison. One last hill remained, and someone painted, "last hill" right on the street. My entire being inwardly screamed, *Lucy, I love you, but I have got to get off this bike.*

The ball of my right foot was tender from all the pressure exerted on the pedal while climbing. My backside hurt from pushing my butt into the seat for leverage on the hills, so I stood out of the saddle to ease the pain. My stomach revolted against all the Gatorade and gels I had eaten. My abdomen ached, preventing me from getting down into my aerobars.

Finally, I approached the helix. Several others in front of me walked their bikes. I switched to a lower gear and promptly dropped my chain (the chain fell off my gears). Some guy yelled at me for stopping, while I replaced the chain. He came up behind me and said, "You know you can ride up the helix."

I replied, "I dropped my chain but thanks." *Keep it to yourself, buddy.* With greasy hands and a re-situated chain, I rode up the helix, and volunteers waited at the dismount line to take my bike from me. The bike was over! I did it!

I ran into the transition rooms surprised to see my parents and Alison cheering behind a rope barrier. I grabbed my bag, headed to the changing area, and donned my running gear with the assistance of my volunteer. My eyes darted around as I took off my sweaty, disgusting bike shorts in the big open room (I don't wear underwear when racing), but my helper wore rubber gloves and was nonplussed. She attempted to remove my cycling gloves, but I told her she didn't want to touch those. I have a habit of wiping my nose on my cycling gloves, and they were crispy after seven hours of riding! Yuck. As I left the TA, I realized I made a mistake grabbing a small water bottle, which bounced in my shirt's back pocket. The volunteers handled the situation, and everything made it back into my bag.

CHAPTER 20

THE RUN

ONCE I PUT MY RUNNING shoes on, I knew I would finish. Running is what I do best. As I entered the starting shoot of the run course, a girl behind me said, "You got me through the last four miles of the bike."

I turned around with a puzzled look on my face. "Really?"

She said, "It was the Bible verse on the back of your leg."

God can work through us without our awareness. The vastness of His reach and plan encourages my faith. He works endlessly and to the tiniest detail, even using me as inspiration for the girl behind me in a race.

I still had abdominal cramping and could run for tiny spurts but then had to walk while holding my stomach tight. I was afraid if I pushed too hard, I would end up doubled over. After a couple of miles, I thought, *this could be a very long marathon.* I drank flat cola at the stations because 1) I absolutely did not want any more Gatorade and 2) my mom says this settles one's stomach (according to my mother, ginger ale, flat cola, and Vicks VapoRub can cure anything).

I prayed for God to resolve my intestinal issues. I mulled this over in my head and then quickly modified my prayer. I pleaded for God to settle my stomach issues when I was near a bathroom! The last thing I needed was for my intestines to reach a verdict in the middle of Madison.

After using a porta-potty at mile six, my cramping eased, and I started to run. There were twenty miles left, but I had logged over 120 miles thus far in the race. With running, my body sets a rhythm, and

I move to my inner metronome. Swimming and biking were different in Ironman Wisconsin. I concentrated on the technical aspects of my swim stroke, and I focused on the course and other riders during the bike leg. However, I relaxed into my running.

I walked up the big hill on the run route and through every aid station to save my legs and allow nutritional intake. My plan consisted of running until "the wheels fell off," which happened at mile twenty. I felt like one of those cheap, dollar store Barbie dolls whose legs can be pulled right out of their sockets. I ran as much as I could and when I felt weak, I walked. I wasn't the only one on the pain train. A guy in front of me shuffled with his head hanging. He had four buddies with him for the last nine miles speaking encouragement while he said nothing.

Highlights of the run included: 1) the jog in Camp Randall Stadium where the Wisconsin Badgers play and my Heisman trophy pose for the photographer, 2) the drum group in the latter half of the race performing and dancing—I was a heartbeat away from dancing with them, 3) the thoughtful guy who shined his flashlight on the curb so people wouldn't trip, and 4) running in the pitch-black darkness (it's not every day I run in the dark).

As I came up on mile twenty-three, I jogged past a guy and said, "The only person I want to see right now is Mike Reilly."

He responded, "Is that your husband?"

Hold up. (*Insert needle scratching on the record sound here.*) This guy needed the medical tent. He participated in a WTC Ironman race, went to the mandatory athlete's meeting which Mike Reilly emceed, yet didn't know who Mike Reilly is? (*And why would I refer to my husband by his first and last names?*)

I explained to him that Mike Reilly is the Voice of Ironman, the guy who calls our names at the finish line and announces each athlete as an Ironman. *Get it together, buddy.*

Then, I saw the jumbotron and all the lights of the finish line. My speed picked up from the excitement. I tried to space myself out from others, so I could hear Mike say my name and then call me an Ironman. The bright lights in the cool darkness of Madison resembled Times Square and called to me like a beacon. (All I could think was, *run toward the light*). When the athletes approached the final 140.6-mile mark, carpets lined the road, and barricades held back the crowds on either side. I did not see my parents right away as I focused on running down the shoot to the finish.

I threw my arms in the air at fourteen hours and thirty-nine minutes as I crossed the finish line and heard my name. Mike Reilly called out, "You are an Ironman!" I cried a little and smiled from ear to ear. My "catcher" came up and put his arm around me, asking if I was okay. Finish line volunteers, or catchers, check in with each of the participants after they finish.

I replied, "I'm not sure." He went with me to get my medal, T-shirt, and finisher hat. He kept his arm around my shoulders holding me up. Poor guy, I probably smelled awful.

He guided me over to have my finisher photo taken, and he said, "I think you're okay."

I met my parents who were outside the fenced area. Every time I had envisioned finishing the race when I trained, I had cried. But, I was emotionally empty after crying it all out on the bike. Now, I felt glad to stop and eat something besides gel and Gatorade. (I had two pieces of pizza followed by a Big Mac and fries a couple of hours later.)

So, that's the story of how I became an Ironman. My finish took fourteen hours, thirty-nine minutes, and thirty-two seconds (along with ninety-three-plus hours of swim training, 198-plus hours of biking, and 109-plus hours of training runs). While I trained, the amount seemed like *thousands of hours*!

Documented forever, cemented in the race records of the World Triathlon Corporation and of Ironman Wisconsin is the undeniable truth: I'm an Ironman.

CHAPTER 21

TODAY IS YOUR DAY!

(The Actual Race Day Plan as originally written)

WAKE UP AT 4:00 A.M. Start making coffee. Make PBJ English muffin (2). Eat breakfast. Visit toilet. Eat salt. Start hydrating with water. Put on race attire: bike shorts, Vaseline, watch, heart rate monitor, white sports bra, TYR top. Put on pants over bike shorts and jacket if needed. Place on ankle strap and flip flops. Visit toilet. Head over to TA with Special Needs bag and Morning bag. Bring water bottles and concentrated Gatorade Endurance (GE) for bike. Check bike set up and pump up tires. Place aero bottle and 2 water bottles (one with concentrated GE) on bike. Stare at setup. Tape nutrition to top tube. Pick up chip and place on ankle strap. Get body marked. Head to swim start. Remove jacket and pants. Apply body glide and sunscreen. Put on wetsuit, goggles, and swim cap over goggles. Remove flip flops. Eat gel. Hydrate. Pray. Drop off morning bag. Get in water. Cannon! Hit watch start. Start swim staying calm and relaxed and not panicking with all the people. Remember mass start practice. Slow and gliding while reveling being in such an awesome race start! Establish a rhythm—buoy to buoy. Finish swim. Go crazy at water's edge! You completed the Ironman swim! Click watch. Have someone help with wetsuit removal. Jog to transition. Take off goggles and swim cap. Get to bike! Lucy! Towel off well. Eat salt. Hydrate. Put on helmet and glasses. Rinse feet. Put on bike shoes. Put on race belt with number at your back. Put powerbars and gels in back pocket as needed. Put on arm warmers. Grab Lucy and head to "Bike Out." Hit watch. Get on bike. Look for family and friends. Ride out. Put on gloves in first 5 minutes on the bike. Settle down after away from the TA. No pushing. Easy rotating. Easy. Drink water. Eat gel at 15 minutes in. Switch to GE. Glide with easy spinning up each hill. Steady pedaling downhill. No pushing. Easy. 1/2 a powerbar at 30 min mark, gel on hour mark. Salt every 2 hours. Stretch every 25 miles. Wave at Verona. Stop and get special needs bag if needed with PBJ, snickers, tube socks, toilet paper. Stop and eat if feeling fatigued. Look for Team Wypych. Start again. Easy. Wave at photographers. Thank volunteers. Encourage other competitors. Race the plan. Verona. Head back to TA. No more solid food. May increase a bit on the bike but no hard efforts. Up the helix to the TA. Go crazy! You completed the Ironman bike! Hit watch. Drop off Lucy. Drink GE. Helmet off, Glasses off, Shoes off, Gloves off. Grab bag and quickly go to changing area. Put on Under Armor shorts or capri running pants. Put on extra or new shirt if needed. Dry off feet. Place on moleskin and duct tape. Socks. Shoes. Back to TA. GE. Grab visor and fuel belt bottle (maybe) and 3 gels. Salt. Hydrate. Run out. Hit watch. Look for Team Wypych. Head out. Easy. HR at 150 or so. Keep moving. Only walking through water stations. Pose as Heisman in Camp Randall. Gel every thirty minutes if possible. Alternate GE and cola at stations along with water. Salt every 2 hours. Go Easy. Slow uphill. Thank volunteers. Encourage athletes. Keep moving. Get special needs bag with tube socks, toilet paper, snickers, PBJ, gloves if needed, tooth brush. 2nd loop. Look for Team Wypych. Keep moving. Gels every 30 min. Easy. Keep running. If you feel good in the last 5K, turn it out. See finish chute. Look for Team Wypych. Thank God. Run through finish line. Hear Mike Reilly call your name and say, "You are an Ironman." Get medal. Get finishers hat. Go crazy, cry, shout, sit down, whatever. You're an Ironman today. Find Team Wypych. Drink. Eat. Beer.

CHAPTER 22

THE NEXT CHAPTER

IN SOME WAYS I WISH the story ended here after I met God on my Ironman journey. Coming to the realization that God's strength carries me through my life seems like a conclusion which paints me in the best light. As with many things in life, twists and turns color the ending. Life threw a curve ball in the middle of training.

Fear predominated my emotions while training for Wisconsin, but my bravado surfaced occasionally. Secret moments crept into my psyche where I hoped to place in my age group and qualify for the championship Ironman race in Hawaii. After a solid workout, I occasionally thought, *Maybe, just maybe.* Qualifying for Hawaii was completely unrealistic, but the perfectionist in me is unremitting at times.

In these bold moments, I contemplated completing two Ironman races back to back (within a month or two). Preparing for a race requires a ton of training and sacrifice and milking my efforts to compete in two races seemed efficient. I spoke with a woman named Bridget at a duathlon in February before the race. While setting up my bike, I noticed her Wisconsin Finisher hat. Encouraging me, she told me I could handle the hills in Wisconsin. She also mentioned she planned to do Wisconsin as well followed shortly thereafter by Ironman Arizona. She wanted to make the most of her training period and experience two competitions. I saw the logic behind her plan.

I had some experience with this during my two half Ironman races. I competed in New Orleans 70.3 with Maggie and White Lake Half with Rachel one month apart. Unlike Bridget, my motivation for signing up for White Lake was a "possible second chance" in the event I did not finish the race in New Orleans. Completing two races based on one twenty-week training period made economic sense. Two-for-the-price-of-one.

Confidence is another benefit of doing two races back to back. So much can go wrong on race day which is out of one's control. With my second half-Ironman, I felt relaxed, calm, and ready. I beat my time by twenty-six minutes, but more importantly, I capitalized on all I learned in New Orleans. I dialed down the fear and turned up the fun. Logic stood to reason this would apply to an Ironman distance race.

During training (while I was mired deep in my own regimented muck), the opportunity for a second race presented itself. I checked through some Beginner Triathlete (www.beginnertriathlete.com) threads online. One member lamented how he planned to race Ironman Arizona this year but was now unable. Another athlete replied to the thread mentioning the Beach to Battleship Iron-distance triathlon in Wilmington, NC, was still open. I gasped when I read this. I heard good things about this race. I lived in North Carolina, and Beach to Battleship (B2B) was less than eight weeks after Wisconsin.

Really? I thought to myself. *Oh, my goodness! I could go back to back this year. How could this race still be open? Ironman races sell out in one day!*

I had to submit vacation requests for my job ninety days in advance. I would need to request the time off for B2B during my Wisconsin training if I wanted to race in Wilmington. The fear surrounding IM Wisconsin encompassed me and thinking about another race wasn't an option at this point. Have you ever faced a dragon or felt like David standing before Goliath?

I sat with this wonderful new information regarding the open race in North Carolina staring back at me from my computer screen. I exhaled. Then I prayed. *God, I have enough on my plate right now. I need to deal with the race in Wisconsin, and I can't look past it. If Beach to Battleship is a race I'm supposed to do, You are going to have to work it out for me. I leave it in Your hands.*

I did not verify the race was open on the official website. I didn't think about doing a second race again. I had enough to focus on.

Then I headed off to Madison, WI, with my support crew in tow for one of the most challenging and amazing days of my life. What we can train our bodies and minds to do is so unreal. Once the race was under my belt, I breathed easy. I was an Ironman; nothing could take it away.

I hung out with my friend, Michelle, at her lake house in Wisconsin for several days after the race. I lounged outside on the dock or inside on the couch, reading and relaxing. Then I headed home and back to work. I checked the Beach to Battleship website to find the race still open. Rachel took me to dinner to hear all the gory tidbits. (Just another reason everyone needs a Rachel. If you race, you need a friend who wants to hear about every move.) I regaled her with the dirty details about my race in Wisconsin, and I mentioned the Beach to Battleship race. She surprised me by her response though I shouldn't have been.

"I'm not sure I can get ready for it," I said.

"You know you want to," she goaded me. *Ah, she was right.*

I need to digress for another moment. First, I need to fess up. I harbored some feelings after Wisconsin I did not share with anyone. My inner critic reared his ugly head again, demanding perfection and scolding me for my lack thereof. I met with my Christian counselor and shared my thoughts with her. I completed a race I thought I would never be able to do, a race which filled me with fear for months. Part of me was ecstatic, but another part was not.

When my counselor asked how my race went, I replied, "Good. But I wish I had been faster." Truly, I had. I am selfish for having these thoughts, but this is the truth. Fourteen hours is a low mediocre time as far as Ironman athletes go. While I do realize finishing in itself was a gift, I am a perfectionist, a competitor, and a performance driven human being. Part of me, the prideful part, was somewhat disappointed.

"Wait. Let me get this straight," my counselor replied. "God takes you on this amazing journey, through something that less than one percent of the population can ever do, teaches you how to swim, and your response is maybe He could have done a better job?"

A discussion about pride ensued, and rightly so. She said I hide my pride well, making it dangerous. She encouraged me to develop an attitude of gratitude. A Fellowship for Christian Athletes devotional I received by email declared, "Power without humility is dangerous."[15] Any strength we have without humility is risky.

This was a huge wake up call for me. Her words hit me like a sucker punch. *Am I really ungrateful?*

Yes, I was. I thumbed my nose at God, albeit in secret. Is being ungrateful and thanklessly questioning God's plan for me a sin? Yes, God knows. Even if no one else knows our deepest, darkest thoughts, God knows. When I realized the depraved nature of my heart, I felt shame.

I prayed for God to squash any effort for a second Ironman race if pride was my primary motivation. I begged for God to heal me, change me. I lay down on my face on my living room rug and cried. I wanted to race back to back but didn't want being faster or better to be the reason. I desired to race for the challenge and because God called me to.

I told myself at the first "red light," I would stop the process and not push past any obstacle. I requested time off from my job, which was well within the 90-day limit. My supervisors said I could have a half-day off, which was enough to drive across the state to Wilmington, NC. I checked the race status again and registered. A few days later, I decided to book a hotel. A member on the Beginner Triathlete website posted that his room in Wilmington was available. I booked his ocean view room at one of the sponsoring hotels within weeks of the race. God worked the details out for me. Green lights all the way.

I discussed my training plan of attack with a friend, and then I went to work. Fatigue overcame me for about three and a half weeks after Wisconsin. I would sleep ten hours and still be yawning throughout the next day. I practiced an "active recovery" for two weeks (working out at thirty to fifty percent of my training prior to Wisconsin), started a rebuild period for three weeks with a one-week peak. My short cycle of training concluded with a two-week taper. My longest ride was only ninety miles this go-round. My parents visited during my peak week, and they sat in my house for the six hours while I completed a ninety-mile ride. What troopers.

As I added Beach to Battleship onto my schedule, I hadn't pre-arranged a cheering section. I could not ask my parents to come again, and everyone else was busy. I headed to the race by myself, which was a first for me. I felt both excited and sad to go it alone. I thought to race an Ironman without any support put the "iron" in Ironman. Really, racing alone highlighted the "God" in Ironman. *Okay God, You're going to have to be there for me.* Sometimes He gets us by ourselves in order to teach us, and I was about to learn some valuable lessons.

As I readied for the race, the difference in the pre-race feelings between Ironman Wisconsin and Beach to Battleship struck me. I experienced tranquility and peace with the second race. I expected some degree of ease, but the level surprised me. True, I was a basket case before Wisconsin with all the meltdowns; the stress crippled me.

Before the second race, I did feel a strong sense of anticipation as I worried about weather conditions, consequences, race outcomes, and hurdles I would face. However, the fear intensity lessened. Knowing I completed Ironman Wisconsin comforted me; I was an Ironman already. If I had not finished Wisconsin, I probably would have felt the same as I did in Madison or worse.

I hoped my increased peace wouldn't adversely affect my perspective on the upcoming race. Fear keeps one humble sometimes. I read my post-race report for Beach to Battleship before writing this chapter, and the writing was filled with arrogance and pride. I cannot seem to win here! Either I'm crying and broken down or I think I'm better than I am.

We all have this insider view of ourselves: our inner superhero being. This inner version is the way we envision ourselves handling a situation and accomplishing tasks. Many times in my life I assumed, for better or worse, that I am bolder than most, a warrior, a crusader, and valiant even in some aspects. But the reality is my life is as mastered by fear as anyone else's. I feel fear, and worry surrounds my life. I cried over a triathlon! Multiple times!

The difference I experienced in my life is that I try to move forward despite fear, or maybe in spite of it. Fear is emotional claustrophobia for me. I did not like public speaking. My heart pounded, and I started sweating every time I tried. So, I volunteered to be a lector at church and had to get up in front of people each week. I was afraid of swimming, yet I jumped in the water and made myself take lessons. Stepping to fear is how I roll. Simply because one experiences fear doesn't mean they have to succumb to it. (This also is a source of sinful pride for me. Good and cruddy at the same time.)

I packed my race bags the week before, organizing everything to within an inch of my life. I arranged my gear into gallon Ziploc bags and grocery bags labeled #1, #2, #3, #4, and #5 to aid in my transition organization. Preparing for this race was easier because I didn't have to pack Lucy in a suitcase or fly. Air travel complicates race planning as opposed to driving in a car.

The day before Beach to Battleship, my excitement was off the charts, and I practically bounced off the walls at work. I finished at 12:15 p.m. and hopped right in the car. Lucy and gear were already packed and ready to go. The drive was lovely, and a favorite song from high school, "Unsung" by Helmet, played on the radio bolstering me. God psyched me up. During high school dances, we would mosh (jump around and careen into one another with the energy of the music). I felt like God said, "Pump it up. You're here."

My pre-race excitement peaked.

Even though I was excited, I did worry a small amount about the various weather changes throughout the day. How would the temperatures impact my race? Would the forecast make the event better or worse? More was up for grabs weather-wise as this race took place in early November. Race morning had the potential to be wicked cold. And who knew how cold the night would be when I finished in the dark? I kept thinking about how it would all come together. I went over and over my outfits and race strategy in my head hundreds of times. I had a plastic windbreaker, tube sock arm warmers, and extra clothing in my special needs bags as contingency plans. I love this stuff.

Beach to Battleship was my first race wearing a Fellowship for Christian Athletes-Endurance (FCAE) jersey, which meant a lot to me. I joined the organization during my training for Wisconsin, and one of the things I agreed to when I became a member was to wear their colors and represent the team in at least one race per year. The race was special to me because I made representing Christ part of my agenda while on the course in an official and public capacity. I especially loved how my jersey said, "Powered by Christ" on the back, which is the absolute truth.

Several members of FCAE planned to race Beach to Battleship, and I hoped one of the guys would give me a ride back to my hotel the next day since the finish line was thirty miles from the start. I asked one of them, Ryan, at the Iron Prayer meeting the evening before, and he agreed. The path leading to B2B came together perfectly. I looked forward to the intricacies of race day and how I would respond and adapt to the situations that could potentially pop up.

I arrived, grabbed my packet, toured the expo, ran into a girl from my gym, sat with her and her friends for the race meeting, went to Iron Prayer with Fellowship for Christian Athletes Endurance, drove to T1 (transition 1), dropped off Lucy and gear bags, drove to the hotel, ate pasta, watched TV, listened to the ocean, and went to bed. The timing was so close that if any one of these steps had gone awry, it would have been game over for me.

CHAPTER 23

THE SECOND HURDLE

I WOKE UP AT 4:00 a.m. and started my usual race routine. I had my race day plan all typed up (again), and I followed it. I wasn't super nervous, but the coffee didn't agree with my stomach, and I threw up. The nausea passed, and I ate breakfast. At 4:55 a.m. I headed out to the lobby to catch the shuttle to T1.

I had called the front desk three times the night before to verify I was on the shuttle list. The hotel van arrived at Transition 1, and I hauled my gear bag over to Lucy. I placed my nutrition gels and hydration bottles in the appropriate spots. Weeks before, I cut index cards into small squares with Bible verses written on them. I punched holes in the tops and attached them all together with a zip tie. In T1 on race morning, I fastened the verses to Lucy; I thought memorizing Bible verses on the bike would help me re-center and refocus if I felt the dark cloud of tears returning while I rode.

I rechecked my gear bags, which hung on my hook, #570, near the changing tent. The sky remained pitch black without a hint of the upcoming sun. I headed to the body marking area for my favorite race morning ritual, which took forever. The temperature was forty degrees outside, so I had to take off many layers to get marked. I spent two to three minutes getting my bare arms out. The body marking volunteer also wrote on my thighs underneath my running capris, though I am still not sure what the purpose of that was (no one can see numbering that's under my pants). Getting body marked in Madison was a more surreal experience.

I waited in line for a different shuttle which transported athletes to the swim start, and I spoke to a nice guy from Missouri on the ride out there. This was his first Ironman race. We shared fears and training stories. The logistics of this race made it difficult for spectators. The swim start and swim finish were at different locations, and the bike start and bike finish were at separate positions twelve miles apart, which meant fans could not park themselves in one spot to watch for their athlete. It made for tricky planning with timing and parking.

Once at the beach, I wanted to see the start line and check for the buoys. There is nothing more reassuring for me (aside from floaties) as a poor swimmer than to be able to check out the buoys before a race. Each race, I scrutinize how far I would have to go and prepare myself for the layout of the course. I try to memorize the distance between buoys, note how many buoys there are, see what color they are, etc. Though irrational, this provides me with untold amounts of security.

A cold, sand path led out to the start and then forked. Unsure of which way to go, I split left off the path and ended up at the ocean. The sky had just begun to turn pink, and I realized how much I had accomplished before the sun was even visible. I surveyed the surf wondering what lay in the day ahead. I headed back to the right fork and arrived at what I and others assumed was the swim start. There was no marker indicating the start, and there were no buoys. Cripes. Thoughts rang in my head, *C'mon people! You're killing me here!* Finally, a boat idled in the water, and the occupants started placing the buoys in the channel.

Finding nothing reassuring at the swim start, I walked back to the beginning of the sand path, where moving trucks sat with their back doors rolled up waiting for competitors to drop off pre-race gear. I changed into my wetsuit and sat down on the curb next to some other girls. We chit-chatted about our previous races and about the upcoming race. The people had welcoming voices and warm faces. I put on my throw away flip flops and grabbed my swim caps and goggles. Wetsuit-clad athletes trudged to the swim start.

The sand was so cold it was painful. My toes turned bright red, and a line formed between the normal looking part of my feet and the red part. I thought to myself, *Oh, I hope I don't get frostbite from this race.* I wanted to put my swim caps on for warmth (I wore two to help keep heat in). I typically wear my goggle straps underneath my cap, so someone doesn't tear them off accidentally in the mass start.

I strode to the water to wet my goggles prior to positioning them. I leaned over and accidentally filled them full of sand. *Great.* I stepped into the channel to rinse them out. The water was so warm! The temperature outside was forty degrees but the water was a balmy sixty-seven degrees. I looked up after cleaning my goggles and noticed about half the athletes warming themselves in the knee-deep water. I hung out in the water to keep my feet warm until it was nearly race start.

The organization in charge put up a big inflatable "START" arch and announced we had to exit the water. The competitors congregated on the sand behind the air inflated START arch. I don't remember hearing the cannon. The only auditory memory I have is of the Eminem song "Lose Yourself" that started blasting. With the music pumping, we walked toward and then jogged under the start arch, and I jumped up to hit the banner. I had placed myself in the back of the crowd, so I would have fewer people swimming over me. Within a few minutes, we swam in the warmish water and headed off to first buoy down the Intercoastal Waterway.

Like White Lake, I enjoyed a wonderful swim. I was relaxed and not in a hurry to finish. I wanted to exit the water so badly in Madison, so I could start the bike leg. After starting the long bike segment, I realized I had seven hours out there and wondered why I had felt hurried.

This time was different. I was so happy to be swimming in the open water and not in a pool as I had been for my training bridge. The buoys were a bit far apart for my taste, and I had trouble sighting. I stopped and treaded water occasionally when the buoys were too far away for me to get a visual. As I went on, they became closer together. *(Part of me thinks I missed my calling as a race-buoy-setter-upper, I mean really. Put them out in a line, equidistant from one another. Is it that hard? But I digress.)*

We were supposed to have one left turn on the point-to-point route, but I was unsure when I made it there. It seemed like there were several turns to me. It's surprising how easy I became turned around while swimming in a straight channel, but I went with it. I asked one of the stand-up paddle boarding guys once where the next buoy was since I could not see with the glare on the water.

"It's straight ahead." *Oh, thanks, that's helpful.* I guess that's what I get for asking directions when I'm supposed to be swimming in a straight line.

At one point, I thought I was approaching the finish, and I felt disappointed I had to stop swimming. It turned out to be one of the aforementioned turns, so I slogged on. I nearly became stuck in the last buoy's anchoring ropes. When I looked up to my right, I saw people climbing out of the water at the swim finish. I swam over to the ladder and climbed out. My watch said 1:08. *Are you kidding?*

My swim time in Madison was around 1:52. I love a good current. We swam with the incoming morning tide that flowed in the Intercoastal Waterway. It was one of the draws of this race. I had no expectation of taking forty minutes off my swim time based on my training, but I took it.

I opted not to have my wetsuit stripped off to keep warm during the quarter mile run to Transition 1. My bare feet slapped painfully on the cold concrete in the forty-degree atmosphere. As I began my run, I passed through a fresh water shower to rinse off the salt. I realized I should rinse the salt off my body to avoid being gritty and sticky for the whole day. In order to help me get the suit off quickly, I grabbed some random guy walking by on the sidewalk and had him strip my wetsuit.

The air was cold, but the freezing ground produced the most discomfort. I felt my feet going numb and worried I would trip over my toes because I couldn't feel them. Finally, I hit T1 rounding the corner into the grass. I meant to stop and pray as soon as I finished the swim, but I forgot in my excitement over my super sweet swim time. So, I stopped near the rack where the gear bags hung and knelt on one knee. I thanked God for such a wonderful swim and prayed for a great bike.

I grabbed my stuff and strolled into the changing tent. I wasn't lackadaisical, but I wasn't rushed either. I took my time because I was wet, cold, and needed to warm up. Plus, my swim time was 1:08, so I could afford to dry off before putting my gear on. I followed the race day plan exactly. I had a copy of the swim-to-bike segment in the gear bag (I know, I'm such a geek!); I toweled off my hair, put on my tank and Ironman Wisconsin bike jersey, arm warmers, and "tube sock arm warmers" over top (tube socks with the toes cut off), which I could throw away. I layered since the weather was still only forty-some degrees, and my hair hung in a wet ponytail. I prepared for the cold which would ensue when I began pedaling my bike. I stopped at the porta-potty and then headed to Lucy, who was the last bike on my rack. I ran through transition, the length of which was about four times shorter than Madison, and I started riding.

The beginning of this ride was sunny and not that cold, thankfully. I may have looked funny in my tube socks, but I was snuggly warm. Unlike in Wisconsin where I felt I was a stronger biker than those with whom I exited the swim, I hardly passed anyone and was passed by only few in B2B. Fewer athletes participated in this race. I wondered if the aloneness would negatively impact my performance on the bike.

CHAPTER 24

DARK REPEAT?

THE RACE PACKET INDICATED THE first aid station on the bike course was at mile twenty-five and would be supplied with sports drink, water, gels, hammer bars, and bananas. After seeing nothing by mile twenty-eight, I wondered if I had passed the station. Gearing up for a certain mile marker but being unable to locate it negatively affected my psyche. Additionally, I worried I missed a turn and was lost. *I will bet the buoy planner was also in charge of the aid stations.*

I finally arrived at the "mile 30" aid station, and thankfully I had my own food with me as there wasn't any nutrition at the aid station, only drinks. I felt bad for people who planned to obtain provisions on the course, which is a reasonable tactic, only to reach the aid station and find out no food is present. I grabbed two bottles of sports drink and was on my way.

During the next eight miles, athletes in the half-Ironman race began to pass me. I saw the half-Ironman athletes on the beach while I swam in the Intercoastal Waterway. Their starting point was halfway through the full Ironman swim course, and their start time was one hour later. They congregated on their beach, and I spied them when I breathed on my right side during the swim course.

The half-Ironman leaders were so fast. One guy flew by wearing a Fellowship for Christian Athletes-Endurance jersey and had been at the Iron Prayer the night before. I cheered! At mile thirty-eight, the half and full distance courses split, so I didn't see any more racers from the half. Things became much quieter. I could usually see a few other athletes, and the next twenty miles passed uneventfully except for this weird out-and-back turn around.

We made a right turn onto this bumpy road and pedaled 500 yards, turned around, and then got back on the same road we were on. Pretty weird course planning. I guess they needed that extra little bit to get the race to 140.6 miles.

My brain power started to fade in the fifty-plus miles region. My stomach felt mildly nauseous. I had worked on memorizing Bible verses during miles twenty to fifty to give myself something to do. I memorized seven verses, including Mark 12:30, Psalm 86:11, and Joshua 1:9 to name a few.

> Love the Lord your God with all your heart and with all your soul and with all your mind and with all your strength. (Mark 12:30, NIV)

> Teach me your way, LORD, that I may rely on your faithfulness; give me an undivided heart, that I may fear your name. (PSALM 86:11, NIV)

> Have I not commanded you? Be strong and courageous. Do not be afraid; do not be discouraged, for the Lord your God will be with you wherever you go. (Joshua 1:9, NIV)

I would change them up a bit to suit the day. For example, I memorized Proverbs 3:5-6, "Trust in the Lord with all your heart and lean not on your own understanding; in all your ways acknowledge him and he will make your path straight" (NIV) (and flat). After mile fifty, I felt my speed dropping, and I had difficulty focusing so I concluded my memorization. I was excited that the special needs stop was coming up at mile sixty. I needed to be rejuvenated.

Except special needs was not at mile sixty, and I panicked thinking I missed it or I missed a turn. At mile sixty-five the aid station with my bag of treats finally arrived. I stopped and racked my bike. They had radioed my number ahead, so my bag was ready for me. I grabbed some candy, took an extended release eight-hour Tylenol, and grabbed Biofreeze (which is a more hipster form of Ben-Gay). I used the porta-potty and rubbed the Biofreeze on my hamstrings. What I did not do, which was a mistake, was put more Vaseline on. Eleven days after the race, I still had the chafe marks in the creases where my legs and buttocks meet. I'm referring to chafing so horrendous it scabbed over. This painful chafing is the primary motivation for me to increase my cycling speed. Less time on the bike means less time in sweaty shorts.

I grabbed my bike and headed out. I said to the special needs volunteer, "Are we almost there yet?" making fun of my own inside joke.

He replied, "It's probably farther than you'd like it to be."

My reply? "Yeah, but now I got Skittles."

And thank God for Skittles. When I first left the special needs area, I heard a terrible rattling sound. I leaned around to check my rear cog while riding but it seemed fine. I worried something was wrong with my bike. Then I realized nothing was wrong; the sound was the loose skittles rattling in the bento box velcroed to my top tube. I decided it sounded like applause. I imagined all my friends clapping for me. It was a nice moment.

The Biofreeze also briefly distracted me for a bit with its minty fresh tingling, but the last forty miles of the bike leg, well, sucked. It was a different suckiness than Wisconsin though. There were no tears. When I reviewed the topographic course map prior to the race, I was mistakenly under the impression the last forty miles were downhill. They were not. There was a slight incline with a big headwind and forty boring miles on the same road. It was not good.

I realized during mile fifty to sixty that I needed to stop eating the solid Hammer brand bars because my stomach churned. My insides weren't digesting the bars well, and the food sat rotting in my stomach. After mile eighty, I could no longer drink my HEED/Perpetuem concentrated sports drink mix, which had been my staple throughout the entire course. Every time I put the bottle to my mouth, I gagged and retched. I switched to candy but still choked down a gel about every thirty minutes. Skittles and sweet tarts in the long rolls saved the day. I also had sour gummy worms and Reese's Pieces, but I didn't feel like eating those. Praise the Lord for my special needs stop!

As the last thirty miles dragged on, I felt like stopping both from boredom and the hideous chafing. Quitting was more of a passing thought than a serious consideration since I would have hated myself later. So, I bargained with myself. For every mile I rode, I alternated eating three skittles or one sweet tart. I pedaled for the next mile and ate three skittles. The next mile, I chewed a sweet tart. I finished the bike course one piece of candy at a time. But that's how life is sometimes; we must tough it out, mile by mile, inch by inch.

After I hit mile marker 100, I stood up out of the saddle driving the bike for half to one-and-a-half miles at a time. Biking while standing on the pedals in a headwind was a terrible waste of energy and horribly inefficient, and I would pay for it on the run. I didn't care. I had one motivation only: to get off the bike.

Don't get me wrong, I love Lucy, but my bottom and the aforementioned chafing burned like a forest fire. I passed more people at the end than during the whole bike leg. I just had to get off my bike; it hurt so much to sit. Finally, I saw the road heading back into transition and soon I skidded to a stop at the dismount line. I jumped off my bike, handed it to the volunteer, and was done! I stopped and prayed before picking up my gear bag. And just like in Wisconsin, I knew at this point I would finish because the run is my best leg.

I changed and took a moment to speak to another competitor. She sat with medical personnel next to a stretcher they had pulled into the changing tent. She did not look injured, but she held her head in her hands and tears streamed down her face. I told her she was an Ironman in my eyes. What a tough break.

CHAPTER 25

THE FINAL RUN

I HEADED OUT OF THE transition area and walked a couple of paces in the first mile up one of the overpasses. Then I was like, *Forget it. There will be time to rest later.* I came up with a new plan. In Wisconsin, my scheme was "run until the wheels fall off." In Wilmington, my goal was, "run until the wheels fall off and then keep running. Run until my legs felt like they would detach from the hip sockets and then keep running. Run until my knees were going to buckle under me and then keep running." And so, I did. I kept running. Kelly Gump.

The first six miles contained vestiges of sunlight as the last remnants painted the sky. I tried to encourage others, but my creativity and energy levels were depleted, so I basically said, "Great job!" to everyone I passed going in both directions. After the first half of the race, my brain computed that on a six-and-a-half mile out-and-back course, I repeated myself to nearly everyone. I tried to mix it up, but when my axons wouldn't fire, which was frequently, I said, "Great job!" to everybody.

Out of transition, we ran on several overpasses near the University of North Carolina at Wilmington. Then we headed through Downtown Wilmington, which has a lot of tricky cobblestones. The remaining route went through a neighborhood and into a park where there was a turn around. I ran to the park and back two separate times.

I strolled through every aid station, and in the beginning I ate oranges and drank a lot of coke. As I said, flat coke during an Ironman is the bomb, and the caffeine gave me a boost. The race packet mentioned the aid stations competed with one another for the best theme, but I didn't really find that to be the case. At my special needs stop halfway through, I picked up, what? You guessed it! More candy. I was skittled out though, but I had cotton candy. Did you know they sell cotton candy in buckets at the grocery store? Ironman priceless.

I ate cotton candy and drank coke through miles thirteen to eighteen. It was a great mix though my teeth were coated with sugar and felt like they were wearing little sweaters. Countless triathletes would disagree with my "carnival style" nutrition plan, but my choices were "eat something else sugary" or vomit. I mean, who wants another gel? After the cotton candy was gone, I switched to Reese's Pieces and Coke or HEED electrolyte drink when they ran out of Coke. I tried some broth, too. I felt great from the waist up. My legs hurt of course, but the run was fun.

I also wore a headlamp. In Wisconsin, the athlete brochure said the course was lit. Parts of it were, but parts of the path were pitch black. Running in the darkness after twelve to thirteen-plus hours of exercising was a recipe for disaster. So, when the Beach to Battleship booklet said the paths were all lit, I packed the headlamp. My light came in very handy on the dark parts of the run because, of course, it wasn't all lit. My lamp was also invaluable in the porta-potties. What everybody else did in the completely dark porta-potties, I will never know.

As I passed people on the last six-and-a-half-miles, they looked rough. I would slow my pace and run with them and ask how they were doing. The answers were not very positive, but I tried to encourage people. I was my usual bubbly self, which I'm sure annoyed some athletes. One guy complained about how he had two flat tires on the bike segment and his time would be off. That's another thing I've learned in racing. It's not about "if" I have the perfect race; it's about rolling with the punches and adapting as things come up. I mean, it's a long race, over a whole day. Of course, things are going to occur, and what makes or breaks me is how I deal with them. This is the skittle philosophy. If my stomach turns sour on sports nutrition, then I eat candy. Such is life.

Remember the girl I saw in the changing tent with the medical people? I passed her while running. She must have felt better and decided to keep going. I yelled, "You're back in the game" and raised my fist in the air. She just grinned. She's iron to the core. *You go, girl.*

Within two miles of the finish, I had to pee. I wanted to relish them calling me an Ironman when I crossed the finish line without any distraction, so I stopped at mile twenty-five.

Before a race, I always feel so pumped up. I hear heavy metal power songs playing in the background of my life. The same thing occurs at the end of a race. As I hit the finishing shoot people yelled, "You're almost done." I saw some lights and the finish arch. Someone yelled, "You did it!" I teared up and thought, *You have no idea.*

God, we did it! I thought as I crossed the finish line.

Back-to-back Ironman races were completely unbelievable for someone who couldn't swim three years earlier. What a gift! Unfortunately, Ironman is a trademarked word, so they didn't call me an Ironman, and I probably should have avoided the last pit stop (World Triathlon Corporation owns the phrase Ironman, so other ironman-distance events are not allowed to use the trademarked expression). The medals also can't say "140.6" because that's trademarked, so they say "140." Beach to Battleship was an "iron distance event" and not an official "Ironman" branded race. The finish was a bit of a rip off in this regard.

All in all, about forty miles of the race were brutal (on my backside), and 100.6 were totally enjoyable. That's pretty good. Yup, pretty good. The only tough part about racing alone or racing with God as my support team was there was no one to congratulate me at the end of the race; no one to ask me about my favorite part. This saddened me a little, but I had great crowd support in Wisconsin, and B2B made me appreciate them even more. Thanks Mom, Dad, Alison, and Michelle.

I couldn't find an area to sit and eat with other athletes, and I walked up to the food table and saw the same stuff which was out on the course! I thought, *I don't want this again.*

I did eventually find some pizza. I got my gear, that had been gathered together from the various locations by the volunteers, and changed. I hung out with some girls I met for a bit, which was cool. Then I took the trolley back into Wilmington and my friend, Ryan, came to get me.

Almost immediately after I finished, I stopped, knelt, and said a prayer of thanks while wrapped in my aluminum foil blanket. God's hand held me up during the swim, blew wind at my back during the bike, and pushed me through the run. Powered by God.

What did I get for my $900 in race fees and months of training? I am the proud owner of two very gaudy medals which reside in a shadow box on display in my house. I received two medals and the most valuable lesson I have ever learned. God stripped away everything from this last race, so the lesson would be very clear to me. He loves me just as I am: skittle eating, body-marking-loving, buoy-crazed, slow-swimming, fourteen-hour Ironman me. God brought me across the finish line, so I would know this. So I would get it. And He had to do it twice, because I'm hard-headed.

After I finished Ironman Wisconsin, I felt like a total fraud. You know, that I wasn't *really* an Ironman. It wasn't that I felt I didn't deserve it; the whole thing was a lot to digest. I planned this for three years: complete a marathon, learn to swim, enter a triathlon, and then finish an Ironman. I undergo all of this preparation and years of planning, then, BAM! In one day, I achieved the goal. One day I was not an Ironman and the next day I was. The switch just didn't flip that fast in my head. However, after my second Ironman, I could look back and see the value of my hard work. It settled in, and I thought, *You did it. You're an Ironman.* It's totally unbelievable.

CHAPTER 26

TODAY IS YOUR DAY

(Actual Race Week Plan)

Thursday:

Fill car with gas. Make 5 PBJ sandwiches. Pack snacks, English muffins, honey, PB, salt and water. Pack HEED/Perpetuem (energy drink). Make pasta salad for tomorrow. Pack ice in bags for cooler. Pack bags to cover bike overnight. Pack car before going to sleep. Pack candles and matches.

Friday:

Leave work at 12:15 p.m. Eat sandwiches in the car. Drive 4 hours to Wilmington. Pick up packet at Coastline Convention Center, 501 Nutt Street, Wilmington 28401. Get bracelet. Attend athlete meeting at 5:00 p.m. at Coastline Convention Center. Check to see if Iron Prayer still going on after. Eat a sandwich. Drive over to T1 Wrightsville Beach Transition at 321 Causeway Drive, Wrightsville Beach 28480. Put sticker on bike and rack in T1. Place numbers on gear and special needs bags. Transfer gear from pre-packed bags into official gear bags. Double check gear running through race day plan. Drop off gear at T1. Head over to Holiday Inn Sunspree Resort at 1706 Lumina Ave, Wrightsville Beach 28480. Check in. Double check on shuttle to T1 in AM. Unpack car and head to room. Eat pre-made pasta salad. Transfer items from pre-packed special needs bags into official special needs bags. Make Perpetuem and HEED bottles for tomorrow. Relax. Sleep.

TODAY IS YOUR DAY!

Saturday:

Wake up at 4:00 a.m. Start making coffee. Make 2 PBJ English muffins. Eat breakfast. Visit toilet. Eat salt. Start hydrating with water. Apply sunscreen. Put on race attire: watch, heart rate monitor, ankle strap, sports bra and capris. Put on Adidas pants, long sleeved t-shirt, 70.3 sweatshirt, jacket, sneakers. Grab special needs bags (2), morning bag, and stuff for bike bag (gels, hammer bars, Bible verses, tire pump, aero bottle, HEED x2, bags of HEED powder, concentrated P+H). Get shuttle to T1 by 5 a.m. Check bike set up and pump up tires. Put multi tool in bento box. Place aero bottle and fill with HEED. Place 2 water bottles (HEED and concentrated P+H) on bike. Tape nutrition to top tube. Put on Bible verses and secure hammer bars. Stare at setup. Get body marked. Head to shuttles to swim start by 5:50 a.m. Find exact start and bag drop off. Wear outer clothes as long as possible. Remove outer clothes. Apply body glide. Put on wetsuit, goggles, and swim cap (3) over goggles. Tuck away extra swim goggles. Put on socks. Drop off morning bag. Eat gel. Drink water. Take 8hr Tylenol. Pray. Find place in back of beach. Make sure goggles secure. Cannon! Hit watch start. Run into water slowly and calmly. Start swim staying calm and relaxed and not panicking with all of the people. Remember mass start practice. Slow and gliding while reveling being in such an awesome race start! Establish a rhythm - buoy to buoy. Finish swim. Stop, kneel, pray, thank God. Go crazy at water's edge! You completed the Ironman swim!

Click watch. Take off goggles and swim cap. Jog 300yds to T1. Maybe have someone help with wetsuit removal. Grab gear bag. Head to Ladies' tent. Remove wetsuit if not already off. Take out hair tie and wrap hair in towel. Dry off with chamois. Apply Vaseline liberally. Wipe hands on washcloth. Towel dry hair. Brush and retie hair. Pull on bike shorts. Drink one bottle water. Put on FCAE tri top. Put on IM Moo bike jersey. Place hammer bars, gels, inhaler and Vaseline in back pockets. Put on race belt with number at your back. Put on socks and cycling shoes. Put on arm warmers (or place in back pocket). Pack wetsuit and swim suit and towels back into bag. Place on bike gloves and helmet. Grab glasses, put on top gloves if needed. Exit T1. Get to bike! Lucy! Grab Lucy and head to "Bike Out." Cross mount line. Get on bike. Hit watch. Ride out.

Settle down after away from the TA. No pushing. Easy rotating. Drink water. H&P on 15 and 45 min, gel at 30 min, ½ hammer bar on the 60 min. Glide with easy spinning, steady pedaling. No pushing. Pick up HEED x2, gel, and hammer bar at each aid station. Stretch every 25 miles. Stop and get special needs bag if needed. Stop and eat if feeling fatigued. Take 8hr Tylenol. Apply Biofreeze if needed. Start again. Easy. Wave at photographers. Thank volunteers. Encourage other competitors. Memorize the Bible verses. Alternate aero and sitting up. Maintain steady effort to TA. Give volunteer bike at dismount line. Stop, kneel, pray, thank God. Go crazy! You completed the Ironman bike!

Hit watch. Head into T2. Grab gear bag and head to Ladies' tent. Helmet off, glasses off, shoes off, socks off, gloves off, arm warmers off. Remove IM Moo jersey and bike shorts. Salt. Hydrate. Put gels and Vaseline in back pocket. Put on finisher hat. Dry off feet. Place on moleskin and duct tape. Socks. Shoes. Put bike gear back into bag. Grab head lamp, inhaler, and red gloves. Run out. Hit watch.

Head out. Easy. HR at 150 or so. Keep moving. Only walking through water stations. Gel every 30 min. Eat and drink at each station. Salt every 1.5 hours. Go Easy. Slow uphill. Thank volunteers. Encourage athletes. Keep moving. 2nd loop. Keep moving. Gels every 30 min. Easy. Keep running. If you feel good in the last 5K, turn it out. Thank God. See finish chute. Run through finish line. "You are an Ironman." Stop, kneel, pray, thank God again. Get medal. Get finishers hat. Get finishers shirt. Go crazy, cry, shout, sit down, whatever. You've completed back to back Ironman races . . . tough as nails, girl. Drink. Eat. Sit. Smile.

Morning Bag:

- Body Glide Warm
- Wetsuit
- Goggles
- Spare goggles
- Socks
- Sharpie
- 3 Swim caps
- Gel
- Bottle water
- 8-hr Tylenol
- Inhaler
- Sports bra
- Plastic grocery bags (2)
- Garbage bag
- Blanket

To Load Up Bike Bag:

- Tire pump
- 4 gels
- 2 hammer bars
- Bible verses
- Aero bottle with straps
- HEED x 2 bottles
- Bags of HEED powder
- Concentrated P+H bottle
- Multi-tool
- Green tape
- Zip ties

Swim to Bike Gear Bag:

- Hand warmers?
- Towel
- Chamois
- Foot toasties
- Sports bra
- Washcloth
- Helmet
- Bike shoes
- 2 pair socks
- Capris
- Pearl Izumi bike shorts
- Bike jersey
- Bike gloves
- Vaseline
- Gels (2)
- Hammer bars (1)
- Race belt with number
- Arm warmers
- Cut tube socks
- 2 bottles water
- Salt
- Nike warm gloves
- Cycling glasses
- Brush
- Inhaler
- Sports bra
- Extra hair tie

- FCAE tri top
- Wetsuit bag

Special Needs – Bike:

- Tissue
- 8-hr Tylenol
- Biofreeze
- Candy
- Cut tube socks
- Spare socks
- Toilet paper
- PBJ

Bike to Run Gear Bag:

- Hand warmers?
- Long sleeved black Under Armor shirt
- Adidas socks
- Bottle water
- Salt
- 2 gels
- Vaseline
- Wisconsin finisher hat
- Towel for feet
- Duct tape
- Moleskin
- Running shoes with orthotics
- Red gloves
- Head lamp
- Inhaler

- Sports bra
- Extra hair tie

Special Needs – Run:

- Cotton candy
- Candy
- Salt
- Biofreeze
- Tissue
- Toilet paper
- Spare socks
- Cut tube socks

CHAPTER 27

THE RELATIONAL HIGHLIGHTS

BEFORE AND AFTER EACH RACE, God showed up in my personal relationships providing support and encouragement when I least expected it. I was very selfish during my training. My focus honed-in on my goal and took everything inside of me. I had little energy for anyone else. But, those around me rallied, cheered, and loved me through this challenging period of growth.

God also revealed Himself for me in a big way. The Beach to Battleship triathlon was more about my relationship with God and relying on Him than Wisconsin. God wanted me to learn this lesson. I didn't realize how much God taught me through these experiences until after the races. Right before Beach to Battleship, I could not escape the feeling the triathlon was supposed to be about God and me racing together, relaxing and having fun, doing what I enjoy. I love to have people root me on, and the lack of cheering section was kind of dreary. Still, I felt the point of this race was different from all the others.

Even though God called me to do Beach to Battleship with Him, I was still a little bit scared about racing alone. I sent an email out to some friends, who had discussed going out of town for a trail hike. I told them to come to Wilmington and work out with me instead! None of them could go. One expressed some interest but B2B was a difficult race to watch logistically, and I didn't want anyone to stand there freezing for the whole day alone, unsure of where they should be. I felt God calling me to do this race just with Him, but it was a hard pill to swallow at the time.

I talked to a friend via text about how sad I was, and I asked her to give me some advice. She told me I wouldn't be alone, and a lot of people would be with me in spirit. She said I would take even more away from this event having raced by myself as this would allow me to tap into strength I might not get the opportunity to otherwise. My friend also advised that at the end of the day, we have only ourselves to support us. In the end God is all we really have anyway. He is the only person who is always truthful and never lets us down.

Eventually, I became excited for this opportunity to attempt back-to-back Ironman races. I saw how awesome God was to bless me with this opportunity and to work out all the details. The thought of memorizing my Bible verses during the bike leg made me smile. I wanted to put God first, even in a race.

I opened the side door to my detached garage on the Thursday morning before the race as I left for work, and my car was totally crepe papered and covered with little printouts saying, "Beach to Battleship." My friends had decorated my car! There were two bouquets of flowers and a balloon which said, "All things are possible with God" on my bike. I needed to clean the car off but wanted memories of this, so I took off back through the door, up the stairs to my house, unlocked and opened the back door, and ran into the spare bedroom. I grabbed my camera and quickly moved back to the garage to take some pictures.

After documenting the event, I went back up to the house to drop off the camera and then headed to my garage for a third time. I took the crepe paper and signs off my vehicle and hopped in the car to head to work. Inside my car on the passenger seat sat a basket filled with champagne, a bike multi-tool, and some glow sticks for me to wear during the race in the dark. *How thoughtful!*

I cranked open the car door, grabbed the bubbly basket, and dashed up back to the house. The container had barely landed on the counter before I zipped back out the door again, down the steps, and into the garage. I jumped into the car, hit the big garage door remote, and thought, *I'm so late!*

As I backed out I noticed chalk writing on my driveway and on the alley behind my garage. I backed up a little further than normal and flung the car door open to survey the concrete. I stood reading what my friends had written, and tears filled my eyes. It said, "Philippians 4:13," "140.6 again," "Beach to Battleship," and "Get Er Done." *What if rain washes this away before I get a picture?*

The race was on again and I sprinted back into the garage, out the side door, up the steps, and back into the house. My neighbors must have thought I was crazy. I grabbed my camera again and retraced my steps back out to the chalk scene. I snapped a dozen photos, and, like a running back on a mission, dashed back up to the house to drop off the camera. Finally, I hauled tail back to my car, got in, threw the vehicle in gear, and roared away. All this reinforced what my friend told me as encouragement. Even if I was at the race alone, I was not really alone. I smiled all the way to work.

Another crazy thing happened that week. Friends I had not spoken to in eons telephoned me. None of the friends who called to catch up knew about the race! They were friends I talked to sporadically, a couple of times per year. Cheryl, Fin, and Pam phoned the week before the race just to say they were thinking about me. The thoughts and warm wishes of these people bolstered me through the race.

Another lesson I learned was not to promote the pity party. As human sacks of emotions, we sometimes get tied up in our own drama. I am notorious for this. I get stuck looking at the world through a small lens and feel like I am all alone. In training, I felt as if I toiled and no one could see. How could I ever make people understand how much I sacrificed?

The majority of my training was completed alone, and, don't get me wrong, I do enjoy solitude. However, when I trained by myself, I had no one to share it with, no person to analyze every detail, including the positive; basically, I had no Rachel. Worse, sometimes it seemed no one else noticed. No one saw how hard I worked. No one knew what I gave of myself because, make no mistake, there was a cost to racing in an Ironman. I loved bumping into Ironman athletes at various events because *they knew*. They understood the effort I poured forth. It's part of the cult: indisputable understanding.

In one of these moments of invisible toiling before Wisconsin, I got a text message from my friend Maria, who said she left something for me on my front porch. I decided to drive by my house after my 5:00 a.m. swim at the gym in case she left baked goods or something that would not do well in the heat of the day. What I found was my name spelled out on my front door in red letters (the letters were made of little Ironman M-dot's, the logo of Ironman races). I found a big bag with the Ironman logo, the Ford Ironman Wisconsin website logo, and the run and bike course maps taped to the outside. She filled the bag with hundreds of cut-out M-dot's, basically Ironman confetti (that I spread around my house). Inside were individually wrapped power bars, gels, peanut butter, gummies, and extra letters of my name to hang in my hotel room. She gave me sidewalk chalk, so my friends and family could write me messages on the street for race day, a photo album, a cue sheet holder for my bike, a small clamp, moleskin, an inspirational magnet, and a massage gift certificate for way more money than she should have spent.

I stood there on my porch and cried. It was at that moment I realized people did see how hard I worked regardless of whether they got it. More importantly, they got me. They supported me. They still do. And it made me want to be faster, to be stronger, and to stand a little bit taller on race day. It made me want to make them proud.

Maria personified another lesson I learned during my training time. She was spooked before her own triathlon by the prospect of people swimming over her in the pool. I told her to, "Run her own race," which has been my motto ever since I read it somewhere. In the Half Ironman, I had to let the "fasties" with their disc wheels just whoomp-whoomp-whoomp on by and stay the course at my pace. Everyone has different strengths and is in a different place, and you cannot compare yourself to others. You can't try to be someone else *(well, you can try but see how far you'll get)*. And what fun would that be anyway? When you see people who are performing better than you are in some way, remember to run your own race. You do not know how long they have been training or what gifts God has given them. Maria kicked butt in the swim, by the way.

CHAPTER 28

IF YOU READ ONLY ONE CHAPTER, THIS IS IT

I SHARED THE SMALL BITS and pieces of my story, so readers could get to know me and understand how I operate. While on my journey toward the Ironman, I learned nothing. I was too fearful, focused, and fatigued. Following the first race, God began to reveal hidden lessons. Nearly every day, I perceived God's guidance outlining a new point to ponder involving my Ironman experience as the months and years went by.

Many parallels existed in my life between the quest for physical endurance and my trek to salvation. During this unbelievable life voyage, I completed the race and accepted Jesus as my Lord and Savior. He became real to me. As I inched nearer and nearer to race day, I grew closer and closer to God.

People wonder if God is real. I hope the evidence in my story will spark someone to look for their own personal proof. I went from being a woman terrified of being in the water, to someone who tolerated the water, to somebody who loved open water swimming, to a person who swam 2.4 miles in a race. Submit exhibit A.

I moved from being an independent woman who used relationships and intimacy with men to try to fill the emptiness, to someone who learned the value of purity, to a partner who chooses to wait until marriage for a physical relationship, to a leader who taught this concept to a youth small group. Exhibit B.

I changed from a woman who barely gave to her church, to someone who gave, to a tither, to a member who tithes joyfully. The exhibit list goes on.

Is my path visible? I couldn't recognize my transformation at the time. I doubted like Thomas. Providing evidence of God's existence through a personal encounter was the crux of my journey. I had to witness God walking with me side-by-side through a huge life event to lift the veil revealing His presence in my everyday life. Prior to knowing God, I stumbled around, blinded by a belief I handled everything alone. The race delivered proof: God is with me, He is my strength, and He has been with me all along even when I lacked awareness. Without God, I wouldn't have made it to the finish line.

God knew I needed a tangible experience and not a cerebral teaching to believe in His presence. He knows me. He is familiar with my doubting heart and critical mind. I would never accept words from the pulpit without proof. I needed to experience God.

Maybe others struggle in this same way. If people require proof of God's existence, then humanity lucks out because I possess such evidence. I own the medal the volunteers placed around my neck at the end of Ironman Wisconsin, which is emblazoned with a saying across it. What does it say, you ask?

I'll tell you what the medal doesn't say. It doesn't read "first place" or "second place." It lacks any comparison such as, "you should have been faster" or "so-and-so was faster than you were." The wording carved poses no mention of "you're smarter or prettier or better." My medal does not condemn me with "you're nothing," "you're not worthy," "you're weak," or "you're not strong enough" as my critic boasted for all of those years.

The medal reads, "FINISHER."

My greatest privilege would be to stand before my Maker at the end of my life and be called an Ironman for God, receiving a Finisher medal from our Lord Jesus Christ. Even as I write the words, I know I will never earn it. I am too selfish, too prideful, too arrogant, and too judgmental (and I've only scratched the surface). I will never deserve it; however, I have a hope beyond all hope because God blessed me with the Finisher medal from Wisconsin when I couldn't have succeeded without His strength. I have hope because Jesus removed my sin and called me worthy.

I wanted to quote 2 Timothy 4:7 in my race report: "I have fought the good fight, I have finished the race, I have kept the faith" (NIV), but I couldn't justifiably do so. I attempted to cultivate a strong faith, but, instead, I was a wreck. I cried. I yelled at friends and family out of sheer panic. I lacked true confidence in God, both in my training and during the race. I buckled.

Yet, I possess the medal anyway, my medal which reads, "Finisher." Ephesians 2:8-9 says, "For it is by grace that you have been saved, through faith – and this not from yourselves, it is the gift of God – not by works, so that no one can boast" (NIV). As with God's grace, I have been blessed with something I could never earn alone, something I could never deserve by my own right. What's better than this?

Having two medals.

Why the double whammy? Why back to back races?

God is infinitely wise. He knew I would have talked myself out of what He was showing me. *It's a fluke*, my inner self would have chided, not believing I could be used by the Creator of the universe to accomplish such a task. I would have let doubts and Satan win as I had done so many times before.

I raced two Ironman races because God wanted to leave no doubt in my mind of His presence. My success occurred not as an accident or twist of fate. The support of family and friends served as inspiration but during my second Ironman race, God cheered me on solo. His companionship stood alone. And, my achievement definitely did not result from my inner strength because I demonstrated incredible weakness. God wanted to settle His love unequivocally in my heart and mind. I am not alone; I never have been. God carried me to the finish. He showed me my life is powered by God.

We all suffer trials, and my Ironman story precipitated principles which can be applied universally. Lucius Seneca quips, "The gem cannot be polished without friction, nor man perfected without trials."[16] And George Herbert says, "Storms make the oak grow deeper roots."[17] What we go through shapes us.

People face difficult experiences in life all the time. My situation differs in one unique aspect when compared with others: my trial was optional. In fact, I paid $550 to enter the first Ironman race. I could have withdrawn at any time. This aspect of my tale always makes me smile. For anyone else in the whole world, quitting would have been an option but not for me.

Mulling this over is how I first realized God knows me. He is the God of my youth, the God who carried me through football, and the God who made me tenacious. He blessed me with my work ethic. He *knew* once I felt called, I would never back down. He knew for me, it wouldn't be optional. Other people waffle around as a "maybe" or a "maybe not," but I don't function that way. I am one-hundred percent, one-hundred percent of the time. God knew the only way I wouldn't finish would be bloody, crying, and crawling on my knees. *He knew.*

People have said sufferings and trials are gifts. I wanted to punch those people. How can I possibly consider my pain a wrapped present? On my journey, I discovered the wise truth in this statement. I want you to think back to a trial you underwent, to a time of suffering you endured. Take a good hard look at the person you were walking into the trial and how you changed afterwards. Your hardship shaped you.

God didn't create your affliction, but He allowed it and used your situation to grow you as a person. I look back now and see God calling to me, reaching out to me in a myriad of ways during the years before the Ironman. If I hadn't been obstinate and chosen the path of sin, maybe I wouldn't have needed to become an Ironman triathlete. However, I was pigheaded and chose the way of the world (to my peril). When circumstances arose, which created an opportunity for my physical and spiritual growth, God capitalized on it.

The same sinful choice transpired biblically with Adam and Eve. They had everything in Eden, including personal, intimate, and deep relationships with God. Nevertheless, they made their choices, forever condemning mankind to sin and death.

God perceives humanity's shortcomings and hatches a plan: sending Jesus, His only Son, to die on the cross for our sins. Jesus opens a direct line of communication to God as He is both God and man. Humans no longer need to go through priests or provide sacrifices to commune with God. Through Jesus, anyone can have a relationship with God anytime, anywhere.

Would God have preferred us to live peacefully in the Garden of Eden without sin? I'm not smart enough to assume God's preferences, but maybe? What I do know is He utilized the situation, the fallen world of man, to bring about a resolution: the death and resurrection of Jesus, to redeem man and thus re-enter into a righteous relationship with Him.

My story isn't a new one. The salvation I received is a carbon copy of the ultimate salvation story written by the Trinity and lived out by Jesus. That's what the Bible is about. Sure, multitudes of stories, parables, and history line its pages, but the overall story is of man's sin against God, God's overwhelming love and grace, and His plan for redemption and salvation.

Coming back full circle, God doesn't punish or burden us with trials. But nothing is wasted. He uses whatever sufferings occur in our lives to mold us, teaching us the necessary lessons, so we may change our behaviors. This growth enables us to become the sons and daughters God needs us to be. *He knows you, too.*

Romans 5:3-5 says, "Not only that, but we rejoice in our sufferings, knowing that suffering produces endurance, and endurance produces character, and character produces hope, and hope does not put us to shame, because God's love has been poured into our hearts through the Holy Spirit who has been given to us" (ESV). As children in a fallen world, we experience pain and suffering, and our heavenly Father comforts and instructs us through these events. The trials I endure are separate from the ones someone else needs to undergo; The choices I've made are different from the person sitting next to me.

In a book I read called *Conversation Peace*, Mary A. Kassian writes:

> "Have you ever faced trials and difficulties and, as a result, questioned whether God loved you? The recipients of the Letter to the Hebrews were facing enormous hardship. They thought that if God truly loved them, he would re-solve their problems and relieve their suffering. The writer instructs them that this type of thinking is incorrect. The ongoing difficulties were not an indication that they were unloved by God. On the contrary, the difficulties proved how very much God did love them. He loved them enough to allow difficulty and hardship. He knew these things would train them to walk in righteousness and peace. The fire of trials contributed to producing this type of character in their lives."[18]

But "why?" Why do we have to go through trials? Why not send us the message on a couple of stone tablets like Moses?

Our trials *are* the stone tablets.

The hearts and minds of people function as God's classrooms. Hardships and challenges serve as teachers during periods of growth, when we make headway on our paths to become more Christ-like. Through our struggles and by God's grace, He draws us closer to Him and helps us persevere. He trains us to be finishers in our lives, finishers in our relationships, and finishers in the work He has chosen for us.

Unfortunately, maturation doesn't happen in a snap of the fin-gers. Nearly nine years later in retrospect, I understand the reality of my journey, but when I grappled with life, stuck in the middle of something big, I needed more than the hope of future sanctifica-tion. Struggle is difficult. Life is hard. As I pounded the course to the

Ironman, I needed concrete ways to stay afloat and keep my head above water. Reflection occurred later. While in the thick of it, I searched for a rope to grab onto to avoid sinking. What can someone hold onto when in the middle of a trial? What rope can they clutch for safety?

During rough times, I found it nearly impossible to see outside of my circumstances. The fear was all encompassing. Throughout my Ironman, I carried around a black binder with my nine-month training schedule inside (*I still cannot bring myself to throw it away*). The black binder went everywhere with me. I discerned no life lessons while wrestling my way through training and couldn't see "beyond the binder." I could focus only on what workout I had to endure next. My trial occupied my entire line of sight.

Everything I learned about my passage to the finish line, I comprehended after the race. God showed me things once I slid out from under the stress and could breathe again. In my toughest training periods, it was all I could do to keep a grip on my sanity. Even if one has strong faith, being mired in the mud of life is not easy. In the following chapter I discuss some ideas, the Iron Principles, which I feel might help others because they were indispensable to me. I derived the Iron Principles from my journey.

Let me make a disclaimer here: I do not have it all together. I need to remind myself of the Iron Principles constantly. God blessed some people with abundant patience and, unfortunately, I am not in this crowd. The road to the Ironman proved to me that change is a process and occurs even when I take a few steps backwards. Chipping away requires dedication and persistence, especially when the road is long, and the outcome is unknown.

Before we begin to explore my core principles of trial perseverance, let me ask you a couple of questions:

What's your Ironman?

What is God calling you to do?

What is so big in your life that you cannot see the finish line?

My words of advice? If He calls you, *go*. Bring all you've got. But don't take it from me; remember Jesus' words in Matthew 14:27, "Take courage! It is I. Don't be afraid" (NIV).

CHAPTER 29

THE IRON PRINCIPLES

Iron Principle #1 - You Are Not the Driver

What do I mean by this statement? After following my story, I hope you realize I'm not talking about golf *(Ba-da-bum)*. The biggest self-perpetuated delusion of my life (and possibly of your life, too) is I retain control of it. I get up each day, I work, I pay my bills, I have fun, I attend church, I commune with God, and I enjoy relationships all because I function as a capable, reliable, and totally self-sufficient individual. Wrong. I get up each day, I work, I pay my bills, I have fun, I attend church, I commune with God, and I enjoy relationships—all because the God of the universe loves me and allows me to.

Maybe some of you rolled your eyes, *Oh no, more Bible thumping.* Well, you're right. It's called Bible "thumping" because human beings have thick skulls and sometimes need to be knocked to the ground before they are willing to change.

Check out the first chapter of Genesis (use www.biblegateway.com if you don't have a Bible). God spoke the world into existence. He said it; creation happened. If a large, powerful Being exists who fashioned the entire universe, how could we possibly think He would relinquish control of everything to us pip-squeaks here on earth? It makes us feel powerful, anchored, and safe to think we are the god of our own world. Or does it? A fundamental concept threaded within the Bible explains how God keeps control of the world, and He works through human beings to accomplish His purposes.

So, are we just pawns in a giant cosmic, heavenly chess game?

No. We are God's children. He is and was completely whole and perfect before He created us. He created us out of love, not out of need. He made us in His image and adopted us as His own, co-heirs with His Son. Romans 8:16-17a states, "The Spirit Himself bears witness with our spirit that we are children of God, and if children, then heirs – heirs of God and joint heirs with Christ" (NKJV). He desires His children to know Him, to know His love, and to have a personal relationship with Him.

Since God has love as His motive and because of His perfect and good nature, having Him in control is more powerful, more anchoring, and more safe. Face it, as humans we mess up all the time. I can barely remember a grocery list without writing it down on a post-it. How can I be master of my universe? Though I may try, the reality is I cannot. I will fail. I am not powerful enough to create the universe, smart enough to understand how everything works together, or compassionate enough to offer my son for the sins of humanity. And I don't even have a son (though I wouldn't offer my pretend son either).

God knows we are not enough by ourselves. 1 Corinthians 13:12 reads, "For now we see in a mirror, dimly, but then face to face. Now I know in part, but then I shall know just as I also am known" (NKJV). One day when we are in heaven, we may understand all the things we did not have the holy vision to see here on earth. He knows humankind's propensity to flip life into disarray, and therefore He makes Himself available to us.

As much as we sometimes wish we were in control, think we are in control, or even try to be in control, God holds the reins. Any attempt to grab the wheel and change direction from our path will ultimately result in some bumpy off-roading to get us back on track. I know this from experience, and I am sure others also have examples in their lives where they took a devastatingly wrong turn and paid the price.

Though I know surrender is tough, sit back and trust you are learning the correct lessons at exactly the right time. Things unfold exactly as they should. If you do not understand the plan, that is okay. That's not your job. Your job is to *listen* and to *do*. Leave the understanding to the All-knowing Being who created things like math and daylight.

Iron Principle #2 - Show Up

Showing up is one of the hardest things for people to do and one of my greatest frustrations in relationships. I believe you need to be committed to your goals and to your life. Saying I am going to do something and doing it are close to one and the same for me. I am only as good as my word. What if I'm scared? So what? Eddie Rickenbacker noted, "Courage is doing what you're afraid to do. There can be no courage unless you're scared."[19] We are all scared. Grab your blanket and go anyway.

This philosophy serves me well, pushing me to successfully complete the aspirations I set for myself. An issue crops up when I assume other people think this way as well. The reality is everyone else is not like me and does not always practice my same methods. A friend will say, "We should get together." I figure she will give me a call next week to set it up. I wait and wait. No call. When I phone her in an attempt to schedule something, but she is busy and does not have time, I know her comment was more of a salutation than a proposition.

When facing trials, this type of maneuver can be deadly. You can trick yourself into thinking you move forward when, really, you stay in place. If you say you will go to counseling, then go to counseling. If you plan to refrain from eating donuts, then don't eat donuts. If you say you are going to spend more time with your family, then spend more time with your family. Charles Bos states, "The important thing is this: To be able at any moment to sacrifice what we are for what we could become."[20] Nothing is gained by going back on your word or fudging the truth. Feelings get hurt, and ultimately, you add to the uphill grade of your journey. Committing to doing something and actually executing are not the same.

We persevere through trials by heading in a direction and continuing to move. Give 100% of yourself 100% of the time. Create a plan of multiple easily attainable steps with each one building upon the previous, whether with exercise, diet, daily prayer, or serving your family. In my opinion, one of the biggest problems in the world today is people do not hold themselves and their actions accountable. They don't show up.

Things are tough? Show up. Don't give up. As Seneca states, "Difficulties strengthen the mind, as labor does the body."[21] Do not give in. Keep participating to the fullest in your life and in the steps God has shown you for your recovery and inevitable victory in Him. Do not fall short of your pledged commitment. But if you do: smile, shake it off, and start again. Forgiveness is always available.

Iron Principle #3 - Rounding the Bend

Sometimes learning new things or starting new activities is challenging. You morph into the "new guy" and suffer through all of the things someone who is unfamiliar with "the ropes" might. In the beginning of a new task, the going is tough because you encroach upon unfamiliar territory.

My Ironman and corresponding training serve as a prime example of this. I ran until I nearly dropped, pedaled until my legs felt like Jell-O, and swam until I swallowed potentially toxic amounts of chlorine. This weak output occurred when I still had months left to train. I was miles from the ballpark of where I needed to be. I thought to myself, *how am I ever going to get there?*

Thankfully, a point arrives after starting something new when things finally begin to sink in. You start to get your legs under you and feel your footing solidify. However, before this glorious moment, the going can be rough. You will be slogging, ploughing, pushing through days and efforts which almost seem defeating. Let me remind you it is called "work" for a reason. Perseverance produces power. But take heart. You will make it through this time and "round the bend."

I call it "rounding the bend" because of the way I visualize it. Think of a learning curve depicted on a graph. The line on the graph steeply rises and then begins to arc as it plateaus and levels out. I imagine myself as a stick figure or cartoon running up the curve as if on a mountain. My little stick figure self struggles and sweats, huffing and puffing up the steep climb. Then, like magic, I go over the curve and things get easier, and I get faster because the trajectory flattens.

Difficult things can and mostly do have steep routes when beginning. This strenuous period happens as you build a base and lay the foundational bricks for goals further down the line. Eventually, you will round the bend and start to feel more comfortable in your own shoes. In training, this process usually takes me two months. For eight weeks I grind it out by the skin of my teeth in borderline misery through the end of each workout. But then everything changes, and my body starts to show the benefit of all my hard work. This is a good day.

Iron Principle #4 - Buoy to Buoy

In my first open water swim, I heard a coach nearby ask his athletes how far they had to swim. After mumbled responses, he told them they only had to "Swim to the next buoy." I stood transfixed thinking what an amazing philosophy this was. Why stress myself out thinking I have to go "X" distance, when instead I can focus on the next buoy? It seemed so simple and yet so applicable. I always focus on this in swimming now (*I get freaked out if the buoys aren't set up in advance at a race!*).

Sometimes looking ahead to a big goal can be disarming and overwhelming. Keep the big goal or the finish line always in the back of your mind but remember to focus on the next upcoming goal or "buoy." You can go only as far as you can see. When you go through something big, feel stressed, or crumple on the floor crying, remember to grab hold of the next necessary step and focus on this instead. Honing your internal gaze is helpful even if you cannot see the path laid out before you. Many times I find if I take the immediate, visible step, God rushes forward and reveals what my next step should be.

Iron Principle #5 – The Skittle Philosophy

In the Beach to Battleship iron-distance triathlon, I altered my nutrition strategy from sports products to Skittles and Sweet Tarts because I could not stomach the nutrition products any longer. We all plan how things will go to some extent. Some people are innately more flexible in personality and in reaction than others. The Skittles tell the twisted tale of how we all need to be adaptable.

Not all things will go according to plan, and you need to roll with the punches. Create the plan and follow it step by step, rounding the bend, and aiming for the next buoy. There will, however, inevitably be things which come up which you could not possibly have prepared for. When this happens, open your proverbial bag of Skittles and adapt. L. C. Megginson writes, "It is not the strongest of the species that survives, nor the most intelligent, but the one most responsive to change."[22] Re-adjust the plan to fit the situation. Think on your feet, find a new route, and get back on track.

A caveat exists however. You always need to keep an open mind, understanding that what you hope to be the result may not be God's plan. I needed to accept the realization when I started training that God's plan for me may not be to finish the Ironman. I only knew I was supposed to try. I stayed focused on my training plan, keeping the goal of race day on the back burner, while paying attention in every moment to ensure I learned what God intended. It sounds complicated but is simple, really. Whatever you are striving, hoping, and working for may not be what God has in store for you. It goes back to rule #1: you are not the driver. Sometimes the jewel is in the journey and not in the result.

That being said, many people abandon ship at the first sign of hardship. *Oh, well, that didn't work, so I should quit.* No. You will get derailed, and you will have to be resourceful. That's a part of success: being willing to think outside of the box to get the job done. If gels don't work, try Skittles. Over Skittles? Try cotton candy. Out of cotton candy? Have a cookie. Don't be afraid to utilize the whole realm of possibilities; you may find a solution that works better than your original idea.

Iron Principle #6 - Run the Mile You Are In

If you run a marathon or even an ultramarathon, how many miles are you running? The answer is one. No matter how long the race, you can run only one mile at a time; you can run only the mile you are in. Okay, so it was sort of a trick question. The truth of the matter is no one thinks about mile twenty-three when at mile two in a marathon. Who knows how you will feel when you get to mile twenty-three! You have to adjust when the time comes. As Emily Dickinson says, "Forever is composed of now."[23]

In training athletes use a tactic referred to as "chunking." You break the workout into smaller pieces, which are more mentally digestible. When on the road completing a 100-mile bike ride, I am in for at least seven hours of exercise, longer if I have to stop to refuel a couple of times. The thought of a seven-hour workout discourages me when the odometer on my bike reads a measly three miles (and the goal is 100 miles!).

I have a trick to make the workout more intellectually appetizing. I break the 100 miles into ten-mile segments. If ten miles takes me forty minutes, then I break each of those into five-mile sets, which require twenty minutes each. I think of each five-mile set as composed of two and a half mile mini-sets, which, according to this example, should last approximately ten minutes. At any given time, the most I must complete to arrive at my next goal is two and a half miles or less than ten minutes. Splitting up the mileage reduces the stress of "having to cycle 100 miles" and makes it more mentally manageable. The biggest limitation to what you can do and how much you can accomplish is your own mind.

While keeping your eye on the prize, do not forget today is all you have. Try to ensure every day you are doing something, however small, to push you closer to your goal, to your "finish line" even if it means resting. Make the most of every effort and avoid getting so caught up in the finish line that you miss the journey.

When you are in a difficult stretch or have a big hurdle in front of you, break it down into smaller pieces and attack them one by one like Pacman. In a race, I try to pick off and overtake the rider in front of me, and I can hear the Pacman *whaa-whaa-whaa* sound in my head. *(Visuals and mental pictures tend to help me a great deal).*

Iron Principle #7 - Use Whatever You're
Doing as a Time for Worship

In whatever you attempt, remember God blessed you with the necessary gifts to be able to attack your goal. Be thankful and show your gratefulness through your efforts. Praying, particularly when swimming, has consistently been part of my training. Swimming 4,000 meters in a pool without stopping is my least favorite workout of all time, and because I fiercely dreaded it, I decided to bring God into the mix. As the pool spans fifty meters in length, it's a lot of back and forth. You do the math. One-and-a-half-hours of the clock ticked by as I slowly swam down and back, looking at the blank bottom of the pool. I had to "chunk" the workouts to survive, slicing them into smaller sections, and I used prayer to help.

The first 1,000 meter I dedicated to my family. As I swam the first length, I prayed for whomever in my family came to mind. Invariably, someone's face would flicker across my mind's eye. I prayed for them for the whole length. On the way back to the wall for the second fifty meters, I focused on some point of my swimming technique: high elbows, pulling water with my hand, balance, or stretching my stroke. As I got back to the wall and pushed off again, I interceded for another family member who came to mind. The second 1,000 meters would be dedicated to my small group at church, the third 1,000 meters for my friends, etc., until I prayed for all whom God had brought to mind.

Likely your routine is not as incredibly monotonous as swimming 4,000 meters in a pool *(the worst)*, but maybe it is. You can easily incorporate prayer into your job, relationships, or into the dark times. In an email I received from the Fellowship of Christian Athletes Endurance, they wrote, "Using sports as a way to worship God opens up new doors for fellowship and communication which would otherwise go unnoticed."[24] This applies to most activities we do or which involve us.

I also completed workouts praising to God and memorizing Bible verses. At a retreat once, the speaker commented on how we always come to God with our needs. *God, please do this. God, please give me that.* She suggested we try having a time of prayer where we only praised God with no requests. If we found generating words of praise difficult, she recommended going through the alphabet. So, I tried it and started with "A."

Heavenly Father, thank You for being so amazing, so all-knowing, and all-powerful. You are the alpha and the omega. You are Abba. I would go on like this until I felt I completely exhausted each letter and then I would move on to the next letter. I ran for fifty minutes without making it through the whole alphabet.

Maybe words aren't your "thing," and you might worry that praising God is too difficult a task. Even so, try it and repeat the letters if you need to. I gave this tip to a friend who was trying to qualify for the Ironman World Championship in Kona, HI. We talked before the race, and she was concerned she would fade on the run. There are twenty-six letters in the alphabet and twenty-six miles in a marathon. I told her to focus on one letter for each mile and praise the Lord as she ran. She said it really helped! *(She made it to Kona, too).* You could easily pick one letter an hour at work, i.e. from 8:00 to 9:00 is "A," 9:00 to 10:00 is "B," etc. and praise God throughout the day.

In Beach to Battleship I worried about crying and feeling down on the bike leg after the episode in Madison. Wisconsin had me on my knees, which was neither fun nor pretty. I sought to avoid a repeat of this part of the adventure. I cut up notecards into six pieces and wrote Bible verses on them. I punched holes in cards and put a zip tie through them creating a tiny flip book of maybe twelve or so Scriptures. I practiced riding in a secluded spot to make sure I could glance down at the cards without putting myself or anyone around me in danger. Riders often glance down at their gears or behind them to check traffic and then return their gazes to the road. After testing the safety, I implemented the strategy and memorized Bible verses on my bike during a race to help me stay centered.

Before telling my "story" to my small group, a friend asked if I practiced my testimony. The answer I did not give was "every day."

Most of the thoughts in this book came to me from God while out on the road or in the pool training. God and I had long periods of uninterrupted quiet time alone together. I closed my mind to the chatter, and He would speak. Philippians 2:13 states, "For it is God who works in you to will and to act according to his good purpose" (NIV). He trained me from the inside out. Take time to still and quiet your mind and let God speak to you, "for God whispers and the world is so loud" (unknown).[25]

Iron Principle #8 - Some Days Just Suck

Listen, I'm not perfect here. I don't have it all figured out. There is no magic formula. You work diligently, you try hard and some days everything seems to work out. Some days nothing works, even though you didn't do anything differently. There will be setbacks. There will be bad days. Some days you will take two steps backward instead of one step forward.

A few big misconceptions are that successful people never fail, they never experience pain or doubt, and they have it all together. No, they don't. I have met a lot of people whom I put on a pedestal only to get to know them and find out they are human. Stuff happens. We get frustrated, exasperated, and exhausted. You will get flat tires, muscle cramps, and lose a metaphorical water bottle here and there.

Another errant viewpoint floating around our culture is once you become a Christian everything is great. Life totally works out for you. I mean, God is on your side, right? Being a Christian doesn't make one exempt from pitfalls. Christians still live in the same broken world. God is not a "drive thru god" where you accept Him as your Lord and Savior, and He automatically blesses you with worldly possessions and the easy road right as the drive thru attendant hands you your chicken nuggets. Life is hard for all of us.

I cycled on my birthday one year, and rain began pelting me. A strong wind ensued, and the drops felt like needles blowing into my eyes. I took off my sunglasses to see past the water, which left my eyes unprotected. I tilted my head, stared down at the road directly under my tire to avoid the rain in my eyes, and pedaled the bike. There was no point in stopping since I was already wet. So, I drove Lucy into the rain for the rest of the workout.

You will fail now and again when trying to reach your goals. Failure happens, but do not dwell on it. Get back up and dust yourself off. Buckle down, put your nose to the grindstone, and earn your stripes. Sometimes you must drive into the rain. If the day beats you up, go to sleep and remember tomorrow is another day.

Iron Principle #9 – CFM (Continuous Forward Motion)

I first heard of "continuous forward motion" or CFM on the Beginner Triathlete website when one triathlete said he wrote, "CFM" on his forearm to remind him to keep moving when the going got tough. No matter how far, no matter how big the goal, no matter how insurmountable the task, if you keep moving forward, regardless of speed, you will get to the finish line. Whether with big strides or baby steps, keep moving forward. Time consistently progresses and carries you with it. Samuel Johnson quips, "Few things are impossible to diligence and skill. Great works are performed not by strength, but perseverance."[26]

John Dewey says, "The self is not something ready-made, but something in continuous formation through choice of action."[27] CFM is true for the race and true for your life. If you cannot fast for forty days, then fast for one meal. If you cannot stand to sit through a whole football game in order to spend time with your husband, then sit through one quarter. If you cannot give up TV to do your quiet time, try giving up one show a week. If you have difficulty praying a whole prayer out loud, then voice one line of the prayer. Charlotte Cushman says in O magazine in December 2003, "To try to be better is to be better."[28]

Frequently in life, people become overwhelmed with the size of the task they are called to. This is where the buoy to buoy and running the mile you are in principles come into play. But sometimes the going gets rough and it's easy to lose focus after being underpinned by an arduous circumstance. Keep moving forward. When the next buoy is not visible, keep moving in the direction of the goal in some small way, with some small step. Confucius says, "It does not matter how slowly you go so long as you do not stop."[29] Keep moving.

Iron Principle #10 - We Win

Keeping their eyes on the eternal prize can be wearisome for Christians when tolerating severe suffering. Having a personal relationship with Jesus does not exempt you from being overcome by worldly things at times. It is easy to get engrossed in our problems and trials and how they affect us. It is easy to get stuck in the pain and hurt.

But, try to keep a part of yourself focused on the eternal reward even if only a teeny, tiny bit. You may not understand or see the outcome of your situation, your struggle, or your life, however, if you are saved, you know how your soul turns out. You realize the result of the final fight. Jesus wins. He triumphs in victory. The battle was fought and won two thousand years ago on a cross. Jesus defeated Satan and death. Boo-yah.

Try to remember this. Try to keep the hope of spending eternity in heaven with the Lord in your mind's eye! Amazing! Keeping salvation at the forefront helps us to remember the right choices are not always the easy choices, and it gives us the strength to move in the proper direction. Focusing on our deliverance helps us to stand up when we feel more like sitting. It guides us to remain in His strength when we feel weak.

CHAPTER 30

THE END

SO THAT'S IT. THIS IS my story. It is not the tale of how I became a triathlete, this chronicle is the narrative of how I found my worth in God. This is a worth I have to re-find and refresh whenever I succumb to the pressures of the world. Mine is the story of how I learned I am not alone and God patiently waited for me to reach out to Him. It is the truth of how I came to the end of myself and realized nothing I do or have done is in my own strength. Nothing.

Does God love triathlons? You better believe He does. He loves anything He can use to reach us. We are an obstinate people who believe we can make or break ourselves. We struggle in life never realizing God hovers nearby waiting to bless us, to help us if we would only just come to Him.

That is the truth, but believe me, this truth isn't easy. God doesn't love triathlons because they are easy. Admitting I was not self-sufficient was a ginormous step. I mean, looking around my home I see my possessions, things I have amassed. My perspective shifted allowing me to recognize these things are on loan from God. They are not mine but were given to me by God out of His goodness. He created everything, every molecule. He is so big, and I am so small.

God loves whatever He utilizes to get your attention as well. What is it? What is your Ironman? This story is not about how to become an Ironman but about how God uses what is in our life to grow us. Trust Him. Believe in His Word. Know that He loves you beyond all logic and cost. He waits for you. He waits for you to step out in faith, so He can guide you and show you who you are in Him. He knows you will fail.

He knows I failed. He loves you anyway. He loves me anyway. More than we could ever deserve or earn.

Do you know Jesus? Have you encountered Him in your life? No one is perfect, and sin is present in all our lives. We need a Savior. To pay for our sins ourselves means death, permanent separation from God. Jesus, the unblemished and sinless lamb, died on the cross to pay for the sins of mankind. God sent His Son to be with us, to teach us, to show us how we should be. He sent His Son because He loves us. He loves you.

To have a personal relationship with Jesus is to ask Him into your heart and into your life. It's to recognize we all need a Savior, we can't do it alone. Being saved wasn't a moment for me, it was a process which occurred over my year of training. My year of the Ironman.

If you want to know Jesus, pray to Him: "Dear Lord Jesus, I am a sinner and I need a Savior. I thank You for the saving work You did on the cross. I ask You to come into my heart and be Lord of my life. Thank You for loving me. Amen." It's not a magic prayer, but an admission of sin and a request for God to guide your life.

There's one last little thing. I hope your heart is softer now after reading this whole spiel. The next time you see a cyclist, please give them a wide margin of extra room on the road. Instead of getting impatient with them, could you find it in your heart to pray for them as you are waiting to pass? You never know what God is doing in their lives.

For better or worse, for weaker or for stronger, for the glory of God's kingdom, and for reasons I will probably never fully understand, my name is Kelly, and I'm an Ironman. Thank you for letting me share my story with you.

EPILOGUE

UNDERSTANDABLY, I DID NOT HAVE a lot of time to write while I trained, so though I started the book while I prepared for the Wisconsin, I did not finish it until years later. After my year of the Ironman, I continued to race. I attempted to qualify for the Boston Marathon, but my race didn't go as well as I planned. I actually put up my worst marathon time to date and sustained a hip flexor injury, which plagued me for over a year.

I raced in American Triple-T North Carolina in 2010. This is a race series consisting of a sprint distance race on Friday night, an Olympic distance triathlon Saturday morning and another one Saturday afternoon, followed by a half-Ironman on Sunday. The combination was challenging, humbling, and awe-inspiring. I had to run-walk the run segments due to my hip flexor injury. I picked up some of my personal best bike splits ever. Rachel was with me, of course.

In 2011 I trained for Ironman Louisville. Rachel wanted to attempt an Ironman, and I was game. We had volunteered as Finish Line catchers in 2010 at Ironman Louisville before racing Triple-T, which was an inspiring experience. Did you know there are more volunteers at an Ironman than there are athletes (and races usually have 2,400-plus athletes)? Handing people their medals made me want to get back out there. So, on January 1, 2011, I started training again.

My preparation was very different this time. I did the required workouts but did not kill myself out of fear like before. I mean, even if I did not finish the race, I was still an Ironman, so I felt much less pressure. Despite this, I also had some unrest in my soul. I was tired. I had been training for what felt like a long time, since 2006 when

I started running. People train for a lot longer than this, but I felt exhausted and needed a rest.

Ironman Louisville was the icing on the cake. I raced with Rachel and a guy from work. I had team shirts made that said, "Got Iron?" My parents, my sister and her whole family, and my brother all came for the race. They encouraged me before the swim as I went down the ramp, and they cheered as I went out on the bike. They jumped up and down with signs on the bike course. I saw them countless times on the run, and my sister was surprised when I stopped to talk to them! I'm a fourteen-hour Ironman-er, I have a couple minutes for my family. My family whooped and hollered when I crossed the finish. I could not have asked for a better race and more support from my family. Afterwards, my stomach was nauseated, but that was the only downside. The bike was grueling but only from a physical aspect. Spiritually, I did well.

After Ironman Louisville, I retired from racing. I felt it was time for another chapter. I started a prayer ministry at my church and, for a while, felt called to full-time missions in Alaska. I pursued Alaska, but God did not open doors for me, so I continued my life in healthcare with writing on the side. I don't always get God's plan. Psalm 46:10 states, "Cease striving, and know that I am God" (NASB). I came out of retirement in 2016 and completed a 100-mile ultramarathon. Maybe that story will be another book.

Did it make me sad to leave the world of triathlon? Yes and no. Yes, because it was a huge part of my life for years, and being a triathlete was part of how I defined myself. Anne Wilson Schaef says, "We begin to see that the completion of an important project has every right to be dignified by a natural grieving process. Something that required the best of you has ended. You will miss it."[30] And I missed it. But there was so much I sacrificed in order to be able to be an Ironman triathlete. I like painting and photography, and I didn't have time to do these things. I loved being able to go for eighty to one-hundred bike rides, but I do not miss the time it took to do them.

I still apply my iron principles whenever I get scared or feel over-whelmed. They were life lessons for me. I mess up all of the time, but I try to listen for God, to see where He is working and what He is doing. It is not about my plan, though, and I have to repeatedly relearn this lesson.

Is another Ironman a possibility? Maybe. I'll have to wait and see what God has in store for me.

ENDNOTES

1. "Michael J. Fox." BrainyQuote.com, Xplore Inc, 2015. http://www.brainyquote.com/quotes/quotes/m/michaeljf189285.html, accessed October 31, 2015.

2. "Mike Dooley." Notes from the Universe. www.tut.com.

3. "Theodor Herzl Quotes." Quotes.net, STANDS4 LLC, 2015. Accessed October 31, 2015. http://www.quotes.net/quote/20556.

4. "Wendy Pope." Proverbs 31 Ministries. Proverbs31.org.

5. Swindoll, Charles R., and Terri Gibbs. *Bedside Blessings*. Nashville, TN: J. Countryman, 2002. Print.

6. "Robert Frost." BrainyQuote.com, Xplore Inc, 2015. http://www.brainyquote.com/quotes/quotes/r/robertfros101249.html, accessed November 1, 2015.

7. "Mark Twain." BrainyQuote.com, Xplore Inc, 2015. http://www.brainyquote.com/quotes/quotes/m/marktwain138540.html, accessed November 1, 2015.

8. Dungy, Tony, and Nathan Whitaker. *Uncommon: Finding Your Path to Significance*. Carol Stream, Ill.: Tyndale House, 2009. Print.

9. "Mary Pickford Quotes." *Quotes.net*. STANDS4 LLC, 2015. Web. 16 Dec. 2015. http://www.quotes.net/quote/16386.

10. Bryant, Paul W., and Creed King. *I Ain't Never Been Nothing but a Winner: Coach Paul "Bear" Bryant's 323 Greatest Quotes about Success, on and off the Football Field*. Nashville, Tenn.: TowleHouse Pub.:, 2000. Print.

11. "Martha Graham." BrainyQuote.com. Xplore Inc, 2015. 17 December 2015. http://www.brainyquote.com/quotes/quotes/m/marthagrah133674. html.

12. Fuller, Thomas. *Gnomologia Adagies and Proverbs ; Wise Sentences and Witty Sayings, Ancient and Modern, Foreign and British. Collected by Thomas Fuller, M.D.* London: Printed for B. Barker at the College-Arms near Dean's-Yard, Westminster; 1732. Print.

13. Poe, Edgar Allan. "Eleonora." *Gift for 1842*. 1 Oct. 1841: Pp. 154-162. Print.

14. Wolfe, Tobias. *In Pharaoh's Army*. London: Bloomsbury, 1996. Print.

15. "Welcome to FCA Endurance." *FCA Endurance*. Web. 27 Dec. 2015.

16. "Lucius Annaeus Seneca." BrainyQuote.com. Xplore Inc, 2015. 27 December 2015. http://www.brainyquote.com/quotes/quotes/l/luciusanna162971.html.

17. "George Herbert." BrainyQuote.com. Xplore Inc, 2015. 27 December 2015. http://www.brainyquote.com/quotes/quotes/g/georgeherb379989. html.

18. Kassian, Mary A., and Betty Hassler. *Conversation Peace: Improve Your Relationships One Word at a Time*. Nashville, TN: Broadman & Holman, 2004. 227. Print.

19. "Eddie Rickenbacker." BrainyQuote.com. Xplore Inc, 2015. 28 December 2015. http://www.brainyquote.com/quotes/quotes/e/eddiericke104722.html.

20. Bos, Charles. *Approximations*. Paris: Editions R.A. Correa, 1930. Print.

21. "Lucius Annaeus Seneca." BrainyQuote.com. Xplore Inc, 2015. 28 December 2015. http://www.brainyquote.com/quotes/quotes/l/luciusanna141401.html.

22. "L. C. Megginson Quote:." *"It Is Not the Strongest . . . "* Web. 28 Dec. 2015. http://www.wisdomquotes.com/quote/l-c-megginson.html.

23. "Emily Dickinson Quotes." *Quotes.net.* STANDS4 LLC, 2015. Web. 28 Dec. 2015. http://www.quotes.net/quote/21993.

24. "Welcome to FCA Endurance." *FCA Endurance.* Web. 28 Dec. 2015.

25. "Silence Quotes, Sayings about Noise and Being Silent." *Silence Quotes, Sayings about Noise and Being Silent.* Web. 28 Dec. 2015. http://www.quotegarden.com/silence.html.

26. "Samuel Johnson." BrainyQuote.com. Xplore Inc, 2015. 28 December 2015. http://www.brainyquote.com/quotes/quotes/s/samueljohn121923.html.

27. "John Dewey." BrainyQuote.com. Xplore Inc, 2015. 28 December 2015. http://www.brainyquote.com/quotes/quotes/j/johndewey132484.html.

28. "Charlotte Saunders Cushman." *Iz Quotes.* Web. 28 Dec. 2015. http://izquotes.com/quote/282366.

29. "Confucius Quotes." *Quotes.net.* STANDS4 LLC, 2015. Web. 28 Dec. 2015. http://www.quotes.net/quote/36497.

30. "Anne Wilson Schaef." *Iz Quotes.* Web. 28 Dec. 2015. http://izquotes.com/quote/286591.

For more information about
K.A. Wypych
&
*Ten Iron Principles*
please visit:

www.kawypych.com

@kawypych

www.facebook.com/kawypychwriter

For more information about
AMBASSADOR INTERNATIONAL
please visit:

www.ambassador-international.com

@AmbassadorIntl

www.facebook.com/AmbassadorIntl

If you enjoyed this book, please consider leaving us a review on Amazon, Goodreads, or our website.

Made in the USA
Columbia, SC
15 September 2019